D1050723

MICHELENE WANDOR was born in London in 1940. She is a poet, playwright and critic and has written extensively for theatre, television and radio. Her dramatisation of *The Wandering Jew* was produced at the National Theatre in 1987. *The Belle of Amherst*, a film about Emily Dickinson which she scripted for Thames Television, won an Emmy Award, also in 1987. Her prolific work for radio includes serials of *The Brothers Karamazov* (Dostoyevsky), *Persuasion* (Jane Austen), *The Mill on the Floss* (George Eliot). Her publications include *Five Plays*, *Upbeat*, and *Gardens of Eden* (poetry); *Look Back in Gender* (the family and sexuality in post-war drama) and *Arky Types* (a novel with Sara Maitland). Virago publish her collection of short stories *Guests in the Body* (1986). She reviews regularly for the *Sunday Times* and the *Listener*.

In ONCE A FEMINIST: STORIES OF A GENERATION, Michelene Wandor provides a unique insight into a generation of women who came to political consciousness at a crucial moment in history. Twenty years ago, in the spring of 1970, the arrival of the second wave of feminism in Britain was marked by the first ever Women's Liberation Conference at Ruskin College in Oxford. These intimate and poignant interviews with some of the women who attended that landmark conference, including Sheila Rowbotham, Selma James, Juliet Mitchell and Sally Alexander, reach beyond public personae to give a moving account of real lives at the very heart of the feminist movement.

Once a Feminist
Stories of a Generation

✳✳✳✳✳✳✳✳✳✳✳✳✳✳✳✳✳✳✳✳✳✳✳✳✳✳✳✳

Interviews by
Michelene Wandor

VIRAGO

Published by VIRAGO PRESS Limited 1990
20–23 Mandela Street, Camden Town, London NW1 OHQ

*A CIP catalogue record for this title is
available from the British Library*

Typeset by Centracet, Cambridge

Printed in Great Britain by
Cox & Wyman Ltd, Reading, Berkshire

Contents

Acknowledgements

'Women's Liberation and the New Politics' and 'The Beginnings of Women's Liberation in Britain' by Sheila Rowbotham; 'Women and the Family' by Jan Williams, Hazel Twort and Ann Bachelli; and 'Identity' by Dinah Brooke, first appeared in *The Body Politic*, edited by Michelene Wandor (Stage One, 1972).

Introduction

On a chilly Friday in late February, 1970, I dressed carefully in a mini-sweater dress, long black leather boots and an ankle-length black and white herring-bone coat. I was preparing to go to my first ever political conference – the 'Women's Weekend' being held at Ruskin College, Oxford. I had heard about the conference from a new friend, Audrey Battersby, who had moved in down the road. Our children had made friends at nursery school, and we followed suit. Audrey's life and world were involved with left-wing people, and her house was the meeting place of one of the first Women's Liberation Groups in London. I began to go to the meetings, and was bowled over by an extraordinary sense of discovery. I found I was no longer alone in my bewilderment at the conflict I felt between wife and motherhood, and the need to have some kind of existence as an active, thinking and working adult.

I was, looking back, that peculiar hybrid of post-war Britain, a 'graduate wife', a strange term when you examine it more closely, since it implies two entirely contradictory things: the wife of a graduate (male), and someone who has graduated from being a wife. No wonder there were so many of us caught in the middle of that paradox, for whom the discovery, and creation, of feminism began to supply answers to questions we were formulating as we went along. The process of coming to consciousness, the subject of this book, was one we shared, and which crystallised (though we could not have been clearly aware of it at the time) at the Ruskin conference as a historic moment in post-war British feminism.

For me the Ruskin weekend was an exhilarating and confusing revelation. It was, I think, the first time I had been away from children and husband, away from my secure home structure, operating as an individual in a collective context. Here I was, surrounded by about six hundred women, all far more politically sophisticated than I was, all seemingly articulate and knowledgeable about the role of women in history, the position of women in today's world; who could formulate profound questions about the relationship between class, gender and race, who could simultaneously quote and criticise Marx (whom I had not then read), and who seemed hell-bent on changing the world and our self-image as women.

In the twenty years since the conference, the world has changed, though not exactly in the utopian way we all envisaged. Our lives have also changed – not least because we are all twenty years on, children are grown, relationships and work have developed or changed. But as part of a generation who took over Ruskin College for a weekend in 1970, we were in at the beginning of a change in the consciousness of women in this country. For me, the most important overall legacy of that weekend was the realisation that, marginal as I very often felt, I was objectively a part of the historical process, and that I could help shape and change that history. Like so many of the women interviewed in this book, my political activism has gone through different phases, but somewhere I have always kept hold of the idea that whatever I think and do plays some part, however small, in shaping the world in which I live.

The process of coming to consciousness has two moments:

the exhilaration of feeling part of a larger group, and the excitement of feeling that one's life as an individual can carry greater purpose and meaning. Choices and decisions become imbued with significance beyond the individual self; inchoate feelings that have no outlet begin to make intellectual sense. I became first, a conscious feminist, and then a conscious socialist. I thought, I argued – I thought of myself as a political being. I believed passionately in the dictum which feminism had taken over from the student movement of 1968, that 'the personal is political'. This slogan had particular reverberations for women, whose work in the home was undervalued and relatively invisible. To be able to analyse something clearly was to show how it must be changed. The feminism of twenty years ago had an extraordinary evangelical power, which it is difficult to convey to today's generation. However uncertain we were, we felt that we were pioneers, visionaries, who would make a world and a culture in which inequalities in the home and at work, social injustice, would all come to an end. Sheer force of will and passion, and the hard realities of political struggle would build a new society in an image we were outlining as we went along.

And yet, and yet. It would be easy and fashionably cynical to look back on our earlier selves and see them as young, innocent, naive. And in some ways some of us probably were. But a harsh, inequitable world needs the passion which the vision of a different, better future carries, and that is why it is both valuable and essential to try and put into words the memory of a moment in time when this vision took off.

It was not an easy, nor a unilateral vision. The women's liberation movement did not just rise, fully formed, from the waves. It emerged, as this book shows, from a combination of experiences; important, if isolated, struggles among working-class women for equal pay and better conditions of work; from women in the student movement who were acutely aware of their secondary status in what was supposed to be

3

an upsurge of revolutionary consciousness; and from other 'educated' wives, such as myself. Many of us threw ourselves wholeheartedly, twenty-six hours a day, into the business of new ways of thinking, seemingly non-stop meetings, reading groups, producing magazines, campaigning on all kinds of issues, working as feminists in trade unions and political parties. A life-absorbing few years. And yet, and yet.

During the course of writing this book, I was reminded of how hard it is for the very concept of politics to account for every single aspect of people's lives. In my own case, this took an acute form quite early on. For a couple of years before 1970, I had begun writing: dense, rather difficult poetry, plays which were put on in some of the many new fringe theatres springing up in London after the 1968 repeal of the Theatre Censorship Act. I had also begun to write reviews and articles. When I 'caught' feminism, I was, like most other women, so involved in analysing the place of real women within the real, material world, that it felt as if there were no public place for the art, for the products of the imagination. I did not stop writing poetry and plays, but I found, paradoxically, that the left-wing atmosphere which disapproved of the arts as merely 'bourgeois', had communicated itself to the women's liberation movement. Poetry, I was told smartly on one occasion I shall never forget, is 'moribund'. I promptly went off and wrote a poem about exactly that, but it did not change the basic situation; art and politics did not cohabit easily in the radical politics of the late 1960s and early 1970s. The theatre of the period was dominated by the insistence that all work should be as 'collective' as possible, and that art could only be validated if it was instrumentally harnessed in the interest of some correct political cause, and performed only to working-class audiences. Otherwise it was mere bourgeois cop-out. I exaggerate a bit, but what's important is the feeling of what I remember. And I discovered during this book that it was, in fact, a common feeling. There were parts of the psyche that even

4

our exhilarating, all-embracing feminist politics didn't reach; art, literature and music were all pushed to one side as we concentrated on the nitty-gritty of 'real life.'

That changed, of course, during the 1970s. The woman who told me poetry was moribund published a novel some years later; the theatre, film, the visual arts, fiction and poetry now all have their complement of women writers for whom feminism of some kind is a proud influence. It took a few years before the visionaries themselves could explicitly acknowledge the importance of the imagination, both in its own right as the raw material for artefacts, but also, perhaps, in politics. After all, you have to imagine some kind of future before you can plan for it.

The conference at Ruskin began to liberate this imagination, even though the documents from it read earnestly and worthily. On Saturday, February 28, 1970, there were papers and discussions on the family, motherhood, delinquency, women and the economy, the concept of 'women's work', equal pay and women's role in industrial militancy and the trade unions. On Sunday, March 1, there were papers about 'Women and Revolution', the myth of women's inactivity, women and the working class and 'Political Perspectives on Women's Struggles'. The closing session on Sunday afternoon was called 'Where are we going?' There was a creche, run mainly by fathers, and some men actually attended the conference; a decision was taken that they could be at the larger plenary sessions (except for the closing gathering), but not allowed in to the smaller group discussions.

Since the first stirrings of feminism in Britain, there had been quite a lot of newspaper interest. In the wake of the student and cultural movements of 1968, feminism was yet another good story, calling up all sorts of stereotypical 'harridan' imagery for women who were discontented with their lot. There were some professional women journalists actually at the conference, though this didn't guarantee

5

unqualified support for the event in the press. One, writing in the *Spectator*, saw those present as 'a struggling crowd of long hair and maxi-coats, beards and babies, the usual mud-coloured crowd, some men, a few old weirdos, a sprinkling of nostalgics, strident anarchists, communist girls in clothes out of Dr Zhivago'. The idea that a group of men were actually running a creche made the *Daily Telegraph* try and tug at the nation's heartstrings by reporting that 'one group of fathers ran a creche for children left temporarily motherless'.

After the conference, a newsletter was produced, in order to keep groups of women all over the country in touch with each other. There was also a small group of women who met in London, in order to find a way of publishing some of the papers. The group's enthusiasm waned, but mine didn't; I took the file of papers, and asked people to write other articles, which I then edited into *The Body Politic*, the first anthology of British Women's Liberation writings, spanning the years 1969–1972. Some pieces from *The Body Politic* frame this book; Sheila Rowbotham's pamphlet 'Women's Liberation and the New Politics', a short extract from which begins the book, was a marvellously passionate rallying cry to women who were beginning to put a name to their discontents. Her essay on 'The Beginnings of Women's Liberation in Britain' also comes from *The Body Politic* and is included because it has stood the test of time very well. It is an exemplary account of the immediate political circumstances out of which the women's liberation movement grew, complete with a powerful sense of the variety of (and often bitter conflict between) left-wing groupings at the time. But it is also a clear and precise explanation to a new generation who know nothing of Ruskin and may be hazy about the origins of a contemporary feminism that they take for granted as part of the prevailing climate.

At the end of the book is an equally impassioned account of the experiences of the 'housewife'. Whether or not it will strike chords with the experiences of today's readers, it is an

6

important example of the way women's voices were beginning to make directly public the undervalued and peculiarly invisible roles of wife- and motherhood, so lauded as women's biological destiny, and so difficult for so many women to sustain as the sum fulfilment of their lives. Dinah Brooke's piece on 'Identity' explores the ways in which we each place ourselves in the world – trying to come to grips with the conflict between the way we see ourselves and the way others see us – a conflict that can have specific reverberations for women who are seen to be 'transgressing' their expected role in the world. The book ends with two more conventionally 'political' documents – the first statement put out by the London Women's Liberation Workshop (the umbrella organisation which acted as a link between the London groups) and the 'Four Demands' which were voted on at the end of the Ruskin conference. These four points encapsulate the way in which the women's liberation movement sought to come to terms with the needs of women in both their 'outer', social lives, and their 'inner' personal lives. Work, motherhood, sexuality, individual fulfilment, are all covered.

In between these historic documents are the voices of women who speak to the present about the experiences of the past. When I first had the idea for this book, it took a conventional journalistic form. Wouldn't it be a marvellous idea, I thought, to trace as many of those six hundred women (and some men) as possible, interview them all, and produce a book which both re-created the Ruskin weekend, and also did a follow-up 'where are they now' survey? The idea of actually interviewing all six hundred soon bit the dust – a project like that would take years, and fill far too many pages to be comfortably readable. I then thought it might be interesting to test the hypothesis that all the ideas and tendencies which later developed within feminism in the 1970s were there in embryo during the Ruskin weekend, so that the book might somehow itself reflect the history of the

7

women's liberation movement as it has developed. In order to do that adequately, it would have made sense to try and interview people on some kind of representative basis – first choose the points you want to make and then try and find people to fit them. But this too seemed in some way too external an approach, and in any case, the large number of books which have been appearing in the past two years, as the 1968 generation, male and female, evaluates itself, its achievements and its failures, have done that job more than adequately. Anyone who wants to read about the history of the new left, about the history of contemporary feminism through its ideas, campaigns and organisations, can do so elsewhere.

This book offers something which I believe to be more delicate and unique. The women's voices in it try honestly to recall and recreate the importance of coming to political consciousness as women, with the Ruskin weekend as both the focus and symbol of this process. It is a difficult and vulnerable thing to pin down; it is very rare that sudden revelations are made in reality. The notion of the revelation, the vision, is a metaphor for the importance of an event or a moment of change, rather than necessarily a literal moment in time. While I did ask people about aspects of their lives since Ruskin, the interviews still focus very strongly on what it was in each of the lives that fed into the moment of coming to consciousness. What kind of women were ready for new ideas, were prepared to take on responsibility for seeing the world in a new way? The backgrounds to each life are fairly different, but two things struck me, as I worked on the transcripts. The first was how, again and again, women whom I had seen as self-confident, articulate and absolutely certain of themselves in public, said that they felt awkward, uncertain, on the edge of, rather than at the centre of, the action at the conference. This was a powerful memory for many and is a poignant tribute to how complex the relationship is between our public and our private selves. Like me, a

8

number of women had had to keep some of their needs to one side – music, art, a love of fiction. In every case, the impact of feminism is unquestioned. Everyone felt that feminism had enriched and enhanced their personal relationships, their work, their political activity and helped make them surer and more confident in the choices they have made in their lives.

The interviews were demanding, moving and revelatory. Because of this, there were a couple of people who felt that they spoke too revealingly about themselves, and therefore preferred not to be included in the book. I think this shows how difficult it still is to talk about oneself in a fully open way – how hard it is to put into practice the belief that the 'personal is political'. It is not just that each woman was talking about other people who could not tell their own story or give their point of view, but also that feelings and memories shift and change over time, and there are some things about one's life that one simply doesn't want to make public.

Each interview is about a real life, about the way politics lives in the memory for that individual; but each is also a story, and should be read as a monologue about the moment of coming to consciousness. Cumulatively, the stories combine to tell the larger story of part of a feminist generation. The rest of that generation, and the ones that have followed, will all have their own stories. I am grateful to all the women in this book for telling me theirs.

Michelene Wandor

Women's Liberation And The New Politics

Sheila Rowbotham

(*This was written in June 1969, when there was no Women's Liberation Movement in Britain, only a few small groups.*)

The so-called women's question is a whole people question. It is not simply that our situation can only be fundamentally changed by the total transformation of all existing social relations, but also because without us any such transformation can be only partial and consequently soon distorted. The creation of a new woman of necessity demands the creation of a new man. The domination of women is at once the most complex and the most fundamental of links in the chain. Accordingly in moments of acute social unrest the question of our position leaps to the surface. Our uprising is the most terrible to the conservative, precisely because it is so important for the revolution. The opposition to the women is always more intense than that towards any other group, and it is always expressed in the most hysterical terms.

Now while the Left has always included 'the women problem' and 'equal rights for women' on the agenda, it has placed them rather far down. There is a hesitancy and a hopelessness about the issue, a tendency to 'if' and 'but' and 'of course'. This is expressed in a curious fear that the subject is 'diversionary'. Of course it is diversionary. It is one of the largest diversions that could possibly be made – the diversion of one half of the human race towards social revolution. Partly the matter is very concrete. It is about 25p an hour and the suicide rate, about nursery schools and legal discrimination. All these need to be studied. But there is another important aspect to 'the women problem' – how it feels in the head. If the external social situation subdued us, it is our consciousness that contains us.

On containment

The first question is, why do we stand for it? The oppressed are mysteriously quiet. The conservative answer is 'because they like it like that'. But the revolutionary can't afford to be so sure. He has learned to be doubtful about the 'happiness' of the exploited.

The oppressed in their state before politics lack both the idea and practice to act upon the external world. Both coherent protest and organised resistance are inconceivable. They do not presume to alter things, they are timid. Life is cyclical, weary, events happen, disaster impinges, there is no rational order in the universe, to the authorities properly belong the business and responsibilities of government. They play dumb and the superior people assume they have nothing to say, nothing to complain of. Those in power conclude their 'inferiors' must be a different order of people. This justifies their subjugation. The impression is confirmed by their inability to take the advantage offered to them, by the shrugging off of responsibilities, by the failure to take initiatives. They refuse to help themselves, they are their own worst enemy. But meanwhile they survive. They are skilled in collaboration and subterfuge. They do not compete, they resort to indirect, sly methods. Like Brer Rabbit they lie low.

Women have been lying low for so long that most of us

cannot imagine how to get up. We have apparently acquiesced always in the imperial game and are so perfectly colonised that we are unable to consult ourselves. Because the assumption does not occur to us, it does not occur to anyone else either. We are afraid to mention ourselves in case it might disturb or divert some important matter he has in hand. We are the assistants, the receivers, the collaborators, dumb, lacking in presumption, not acting consciously upon the external world, much given to masochism. We become sly – never trust a woman – we seek revenge, slighted we are terrible; we are trained for subterfuge, we are natural creatures of the underground. Within us there are great gullies of bitterness, but they do not appear on the surface. Our wrapped-up consciousness creeps along the sewers, occasionally emerging through a manhole. After death, hag-like spirits roam the earth, the symbols of frustrated unfulfilled desires. But in life our spirits are contained.

The Beginnings of Women's Liberation in Britain

Sheila Rowbotham

In the autumn of 1968 vague rumours of the women's movement in America and Germany reached Britain. We had only a
hazy idea of what was going on. No one I knew then had
actually read anything which had been produced by the
women's groups. All we knew was that women had met together
and had encountered opposition within the left. Some of the
ideas discussed in Germany and America had already percolated
through. In the diary I kept during 1967 there are persistent
references to incidents I'd seen and books I'd read from a
women's liberation point of view. I can remember odd conversations with women who were friends of mine, and particular
very intense moments when I was hurt and made angry by the
attitudes of men on the left. But it was still at an intellectual level.
We didn't think of meeting consciously as a group, far less of
forming a movement. We were floundering around. The organisational initiative came from elsewhere.

A women's rights group formed in Hull in the spring of 1968
around the campaign led by Lil Bilocca and the fishermen's

14

wives to improve the safety of trawlers after two ships had been lost in bad weather in January 1968. Mrs Bilocca had fantastic courage and resolution. She was ready to take anyone on. She said if the ships sailed without proper safety precautions 'I shall be aboard and they will have to move me by force'. It was unusual to see a woman fighting publicly and speaking, and men on the left listening with respect, tinged admittedly with a touch of patronage. The response from the trawler owners was predictable, a combination of class insolence and sexual contempt. Said the secretary of the Hull Trawler Officers Guild, 'Mrs Bilocca has not enhanced the image the public may have of fishermen's wives. . . . The idea of forming a women's committee to fight battles for the men is to my mind completely ludicrous.'

The wives of the fishermen and particularly Lil Bilocca encountered hostility also from some of the other women and men in the fishing community. Mrs Bilocca received threatening letters and couldn't get a job. Out of this opposition and the connections it had also for left middle-class women came the Equal Rights Group in Hull. Though the working class women drifted off, it continued as a group and later organised a meeting for all the sixth-formers in the town on women's liberation.

When the sewing machinists at Dagenham, led by Rose Boland, brought Fords to a halt, it acted in a similar way to make women on the left feel they could do something. The women wanted the right to work on machines in C grade because although they had to pass a test on these machines they could only work on the lower-paid grades. This developed into a demand for equal pay. It lasted for three weeks and received the full glare of publicity; the papers called it the 'Petticoat Strike' and the women received the usual sexual banter which any action taken by women provokes. It imposed a great strain on their personal lives; Rose Boland said she hardly ever saw her husband and son in the whole three weeks, 'they never knew whether I was in or out'. The strike came out of the particular conditions in Dagenham; in Halewood the women weren't so interested. Rose Boland believed that this was

15

because 'they've got a different way of life up there really, up there the man is the boss. Not so much now with the younger generation but more with people of my age. The youngsters of today won't have it, they want it on an equal basis'.

The Fords strike sent a tremor of hope through the trade-union movement. Women who had fought hopelessly at TUC meetings for equal pay took heart again. There followed a period of industrial militancy among women workers which has only been sporadically chronicled in the socialist press, and has never been seriously studied. Rose Boland was undoubtedly right when she said, 'I think the Ford women have definitely shaken the women of the country'.

Out of the Fords strike came a trade-union organisation for women's equal pay and equal rights called the National Joint Action Committee for Women's Equal Rights, which organised a demonstration of trade-union women for equal pay in May 1969. NJACWER's membership was mainly older trade-union men and women in the Labour Party and Communist Party, who were often heavily involved in committee work. It remained rather an official body which had an impressive existence on paper but only tentatively got off the ground in practice after the demonstration.

A small group of women in a Trotskyist organisation, the International Marxist Group, went to the early NJACCWER meetings and helped to set up the first NJACCWER groups. Interest in the position of women had appeared earlier when IMG was called the Nottingham Group. But it was the initiative of the trade-union women which meant the IMG women could raise the topic in their organisation without being dismissed. Although they had some connections with the American move-ment, their approach to the position of women was a traditional Marxist one. They were terrified of being called feminists at first. In Nottingham and London Socialist Woman groups were formed and produced a journal, *Socialist Woman*. Not all the women in Socialist Woman groups were in IMG, but the journal had a broad Marxist perspective. The first number announced,

'We are not anti-male, a charge often thrown at those concerned with the woman question. We are opposed to private property, the alienation of labour under capitalism, the exploitation of the entire working class, we are opposed to men who do the "gaffer's" job and assist him to do the dirty on women workers – whether in the home or in industry'. (*Socialist Woman*, February 1969)

The Fords women also helped to make the question of women's specific oppression easier to discuss on the left. At first the men would only admit that working-class women had anything to complain about. Very defensively at first and with no theoretical justification, only our own feelings, women on and around the student left began to try and connect these feelings to the Marxism they had accepted only intellectually before. Out of the first faltering attempts at these connections came an edition of the revolutionary paper *Black Dwarf* in January 1969. There were articles about being an unsupported mother, how to get contraceptive advice, women in trade unions, and Marxism and psychology (by a man) and a thing by me trying to relate how you encountered sexual humiliation to Marxism. They all appear very obvious now, but at the time it was very hard to make the connections, and just having something down on paper meant you didn't feel either a hopeless bitter rage or as if you were a completely neurotic freak. I remember one left man coming up to me and with a pitying air saying he supposed it had helped me to express my personal problems but it was nothing to do with socialism.

Completely separately another group had formed in London. They were predominantly American and in their mid-20s. Some of them had been active in Camden Vietnam Solidarity Campaign, most of them had husbands who were very deeply involved in revolutionary politics. Many of them too had small children and felt very isolated both as housewives and as foreigners. They started to meet in Tufnell Park and were later to have an extremely important influence, particularly on the London Workshop.

'It was tremendously exciting. We felt like we were breaking through our conditioning and learning new things each week. Maybe small groups have this same experience now, but I think there was probably more tension and emotion because of the newness of it all – no one else seemed to have heard of Women's Liberation – we were freaks. I used to be exhausted and exhilarated after meetings and used to lie awake thinking – couldn't stop. We argued a lot with each other. We were mostly political, mostly not marxists because our experience and identification was American new left of the first half of the 60s type, ie before Marx and Lenin. I'm glad it was that way. We all felt Women's Liberation at a gut level and for me at least it led to reading (starting to anyway) Marx and Lenin . . . because we were confused and unclear in some aspects of our politics the way was clear for us to admit the truth and feelings of Women's Liberation into ourselves and then try to work it all out . . . We were really concerned with whether we could change our lives at all in view of our involvement in Women's Liberation. We wanted to be able to break down the barriers between private personal life and public political life. We admired and discussed Helke Sanders' statement to the German SDS conference. That piece also influenced our attempts to organise something for our own children and we met a number of times as adults and as adults with children with German SDS people in Golders Green'. (Letter from member of the original Tufnell Park group, June 1971)

Shortly after the issue of *Black Dwarf* came out, the women at Essex University arranged a discussion of women's liberation as part of a revolutionary festival there. The atmosphere of Essex at the time was fraught with impotent isolated revolt. The festival was broken up continually by a group of students who regarded any structured discussion as a violation of their 'freedom'. The meeting on women's liberation was in a lecture hall. There was a very tense feeling around. A man carried a girl in on his back. Someone messed about with the lights. Branka Hoare, who was connected with the *New Left Review*, started to read a paper in a very quiet, nervous-sounding voice. There were occasional

18

interruptions and then a curious silent coalescing of the women in the room. We felt a most profound collective urgency. But we couldn't communicate it very well in the discussion that followed.

At various times it seemed as if the meeting would go over the edge and end in acrimony and ridicule. A very clear intervention by a man from the German SDS describing what had happened in Frankfurt and warning the men not to make the same mistakes was important because it prevented it from being just a women's case against the men. For a moment the women's resentment focussed on a man who made a speech about political priorities. He said very self-importantly that in a revolutionary movement you couldn't waste time on trivia, and the fact was that women simply weren't capable of writing leaflets. In the smaller meeting we held later a girl hissed venomously through her teeth, 'I always change his fucking leaflets when I type them anyway'. When we held the little meeting we didn't have any definite commitment to being an all-woman group. A few men came and could be said to have played a historic role. One was a ponderous and patriarchal Maoist who lectured us endlessly on marxism-leninism, another was a twitchy young man who said we were like a mothers' tea-party because we kept giggling.

The next meeting we held we decided not to have men because we wanted to work things out amongst ourselves. One man came in fact to this meeting and kept saying we must have a theoretical reason to exclude him. We said we didn't have one but we were fed up with being told by men what we ought to think about ourselves and them. This meeting was very long and rambling. People were going on about shopping hours and nurseries and Mao on consciousness. There was a girl from the SDS there who told us about the Kinderladen, and people from the Tufnell Park group. It didn't occur to us to form discussion groups just to talk. We were very grandiose about doing things immediately. I don't think any of us realised we were starting a movement.

Three permanent groups started, one in Essex and two in

London, including the Tufnell Park group. The first newsletter came out in May. The next issue was called *Harpies Bizarre* and reported response from leafletting the equal pay demonstration, and the formation of a group in Peckham.

> 'Meeting of a group of housewives and students from Morley College. The group grew out of Juliet Mitchell's classes at the Anti-University.' (*Harpies Bizarre*, no. 2, June 1969)

The third newsletter was called *Shrew* and the name stuck, with the principle established that the editing should pass from group to group. This issue reflected the disparate influences which went into the London Workshop. It included accounts of meetings with older feminists and a vehement denunciation of the Maoists in the Revolutionary Socialist Students Federation who had criticised feminism.

> 'I do not intend to ask permission from Peking before proceeding. I do not intend to neurotically consult Marxengelslenin before baring my teeth or my teats. I do not intend to give ladylike (read suck ass) reassurance to radical chauvinists during the course of this struggle, even if it means losing their friendship (ie patronage)'. (*Shrew*, no.3, July 1969)

But in the same issue Irene Fick wrote,

> 'While fighting for economic and social equality in general, under the present capitalist society, women must oppose male chauvinism and domination in personal life'. Only with the ending of 'class society' was women's liberation possible. The Workshop had from the start a cheerful eclecticism. Any woman was welcome, 'communists, along with maoists, trotskyists, syndicalists, Seventh Day Adventurists, nuns, anarchists, Labour Party members, etc., in short feminists'. (Irene Fick)

The women who came in fact tended to be young housewives who were only mildly left-wing. But there was at least one link with an older feminist tradition. A woman of 78 who was a pensioner wrote in the September *Shrew*,

20

'It has been pointed out that no exercise of power is ever relinquished voluntarily. It always has to be overcome by overwhelming force – not necessarily physical force, but the force of public opinion. In my view it is futile for women to rely on men to fight their battle for them. They must do it themselves – even at the risk of being dubbed "battle-axes" or any of the traditional moves to discourage revolt.'

When the Tufnell Park group produced *Shrew* in October 69 they raised questions which have continued to be discussed by many other groups since. They presented them in conversational form. They hinged on the old problem of how explicit the aims of any organisation on the left must be.

'Do we present ourselves as socialists? I think we should work with women in any action which is relevant to them as women, not necessarily as socialists.'
'No, this could lead to manipulating people: it is using a common problem to mobilise people under false pretences. To organise as many people as possible at the expense of hiding half our ideas is dangerous and is ultimately going to backfire.'
'We have to make it explicit from the start that women's common problems can only be solved by means of a radical social change in the framework of the existing system.'
'If we had a mass movement of women who were aware of their common problem, but never got beyond that, I wouldn't be interested in them as a political movement. Women have to understand the causes of their oppression . . . Women have to believe that revolution is necessary for themselves, not just for some abstract group of people called the working class. They have to feel that they are part of it, and that they can participate.'

The Workshop remained open and theoretically only vaguely defined. There was an instinctive emphasis on politics from below, a trust in personal experience, a suspicion of theory, and a belief in the small group as a basic organising point.

By this time other groups had started in other towns. There was a Socialist Woman group in Nottingham, for example, and a group in Coventry which had originated in the university but spread to include some working-class women on a local council estate. In autumn 1969 a few of us held a completely informal meeting at Ruskin College in Oxford during a meeting on working-class history, to suggest having a similar meeting on women's history. An American girl from Coventry who was in International Socialism said we shouldn't have an academic history meeting but a general meeting on women's liberation. We planned this for February 1970 and met several times in London to organise, though a small group of women in Oxford bore the main strain.

We thought perhaps a hundred women could come. In fact more than 500 people turned up, 400 women, 60 children and 40 men, and we had to go into the Oxford Union buildings because Ruskin was too small. I'd never seen so many women looking so confident in my life before. The night we arrived, they kept pouring into Ruskin with bags and babies. The few men around looked rather like women look at most large predominantly male meetings – rather out on a limb. The reports on the Friday evening session were the most interesting, because you felt part of a movement for the first time. This was captured again in the Saturday evening workshops but tended to go during the very large open sessions when there were papers on the family, crime, work, and history. The National Co-ordinating Committee was set up with a very loose structure in order to circulate information round the groups. (This was dissolved at the national conference at Skegness in September 1971 and replaced by a more workable structure.)

It was really from the Oxford conference in February 1970 that a movement could be said to exist. The earliest activities had been propagandist and educational, speaking in schools, leafletting the Ideal Home Exhibition, demonstrating outside the Miss World competition in 1969. During 1970 all the new groups faced the problem of sudden growth, combined with rapid turnover of membership. Inevitably this forced the organisation of groups, informally, upon a few women who came regularly. There were very few women with experience in organisational initiative. Even the ones in political groups had tended to take action on the cue of the men. We went off into leafletting-type political work very quickly, often as a result of the enthusiasm of apolitical women to do something, and the guilt impressed on the Marxist women about simply talking to other middle-class women.

In contrast to America where the movement in some places became very inward-turning because of exhaustive conscious-ness-raising, in England we rather over-reacted against this and have never built up the independent strength they achieved. We have not solved the problem of translating the personal solidarity of the small group into external action either. We made obvious beginners' mistakes. The Sheffield group, for instance, gave out leaflets on contraception at a factory gate at 6 in the morning. Not surprisingly, the women teased them mercilessly. 'Sex at this time in the morning. You must be joking.' York organised a meeting on equal pay without contacting trade union women thoroughly first. Nobody came.

Although the movement is nationally committed to four demands, equal pay, improved education, 24-hour nurseries, free contraception and abortion on demand, action for these, apart from the demonstration of March 1971, has been very localised and groups have taken up issues as they came up.

The Liverpool group for instance was involved in opposing the Catholic lobby for making abortion illegal. Birmingham worked with the Schools Action Union to support the woman school teacher who was sacked for appearing masturbating in a sex education film for schools. The initiative for the four national campaigns came from the Socialist Woman groups and the Women's Liberation Front (Maoist). They were concerned that the movement would disintegrate into 'psychological' discus-sions of problems. The difficulty about these campaigns was that they didn't grow out of real organisational developments from below. They floated down from documents prepared by little groups. They are handy as answers for us when we don't know how to reply to the question 'But what do you want?'. But they

23

did not come from any understanding of how our movement had come into being and what our strategy should be. Instead we found ourselves caught between being a new movement which is still essentially for mutual education and propaganda and, at the same time, a movement trying to organise without any explicit theory of where our strength lies within capitalism and thus of how we can act, how we relate to other left groups, what is distinct about the ideas in women's liberation. It is true, of course, that you learn too through doing. But it takes time to collect and circulate information and experience from which to draw any conclusions. We are only just beginning to establish ways of getting information through.

Although the first groups tended to consist of students, later on they became less important. The women who have joined tend to be still predominantly middle class, in their twenties and thirties, housewives and white collar workers. A few groups include men – Liverpool and Leeds for example. The real growth came after the demonstration in March 1971. Groups have formed more slowly in Scotland and Wales. Many of the women who join have no previous political experience and only very vague political ideas.

All the revolutionary left organisations have had an awkward relationship to women's liberation. The personal and emotional emphasis and its middle-class membership put them off. But its growth and its appeal directly to the women in left organisations, often almost despite themselves and against all their training, makes it difficult to ignore. From the start a small group of Maoists, almost exclusively based in the London area (Women's Liberation Front, later Union of Women for Liberation), and the IMG women in Socialist Woman groups, of which there are several throughout the country, have each worked as an organised political tendency in Women's Liberation. The Maoists have been the least successful. Their initial strength lay in their zeal for attending committee meetings, and their prolific duplication of unintelligible documents which terrified people into believing they must be very high-powered because they were so difficult

24

to understand. The IMG women have worked more flexibly and have consequently gained more support. They have had a strong activist emphasis which has attracted people, and they stressed the importance of working with women in industry: their meetings are relatively formal. It is evident, however, that there are certain tensions between being members of an international Trotskyist organisation and being members of the unaffiliated Socialist Woman groups, whose members are united simply by accepting the name 'Socialist'. This has already produced a split in the Socialist Woman groups, and it raises the whole question of an organisation with its politics clearly formulated working as a tendency in an ill-defined movement.

International Socialism, a semi-Trotskyist group, and the Communist Party haven't encountered this problem as explicit tendencies because their members entered women's liberation as individuals without official backing. The official attitude in IS has shifted from joking incredulity to grudging support. The change has been a result of pressure from IS women, at first only a handful, mainly in Coventry and London, who argued for women's liberation from the start. The initial response was to OK political activity with working-class women and an admission that women weren't playing their full role in the organisation of IS. But as more women got involved they have started to push the implications of women's liberation home. At the first IS women's conference in summer 1971 the question of how revolutionary organisations should relate to movements like Women's Liberation, of the connection between sexuality and personal attitudes to political consciousness, and of the lack of any marxist analysis to explain the position of women who work as housewives were raised.

Within the Communist Party there was more attention to women's issues, and more of a tradition of a limited kind of emancipation, than in the more recently formed Marxist groups. There is a women's organisation and a women's organiser in the Party. But the official line tended to favour safe questions – equal pay, nurseries – and avoid any discussion of the family or

25

sexuality. When a small group of young women in the Communist Party raised these issues they provoked uproar but also gained quite a lot of support, and controversy trickled into the *Morning Star*.

Unfortunately, most working-class and trade-union women know about women's liberation mainly from the media, except in particular cases where people from Women's Liberation have supported them, as in the Night Cleaners' Campaign which started in autumn 1970. The only way their suspicion can be broken down is by us explaining ourselves and giving them practical support. At present women's liberation as a movement is very mysterious to them. They have noticed it seems to grow, but it rarely enters their lives in the shape of people they know. Many of them have been campaigning for equal pay and nurseries for years and feel understandably suspicious of publicity suddenly given to young, middle-class women. At the same time, women's liberation has communicated itself rather as a symbolic slogan of defiance, particularly to young working-class girls.

Sandra Peers, who is in IS, describes a discussion at a TUC school in Newcastle on equal pay when women's liberation was raised.

'All the women had doubts about it, and some were very hostile. By the end most were won over, though I doubt if any of them will ever join women's liberation organisations for reasons of time as much as anything ... Their chief objections were the glorification of outside work as a means of liberation, the anti-men image and the bra-burning image – most of which derive from TV interviews rather than from actual positions taken within women's liberation. The chief argument that won them over was that it is largely the attitudes of women (and, to a lesser extent, men) to women's role in society that holds back militancy, and most of them eventually agreed that women's liberation had at least got a useful propagandist role to play in getting at these attitudes. One thing that rather surprised me was the extent to which the women accepted without any show of concern that

26

monogamous marriage and the present family structure are on the way out, and supported abortion on demand. About half of them agreed with it.' (Report on a TUC weekend school on equal pay, 'IS Women's Newsletter')

It has been easier in America for women's liberation to relate and develop in practical activity with other movements. In Britain the student movement was collapsing as women's liberation started, and the Vietnam Solidarity Campaign was already dead. The real political initiative has come from the labour movement, in the struggle against the Industrial Relations Act, and opposition to unemployment and wage cuts, in which the Communist Party had the most influence but where even the small revolutionary groups were better equipped to intervene than women's liberation. The structure of women's liberation serves an educational propagandist function but is difficult to mobilise. Also it is almost impossible to act in a concerted way without any clear agreement of what your aims are. The fact that working-class opposition to the Tories' economic policies is predominantly male makes it more removed from the experience of women who are not left-wing in women's liberation. Accordingly the response has been limited to supporting demonstrations, organising meetings to discuss the Industrial Relations Act, or trying to communicate to working-class housewives about trade union rights and rising prices. Particularly the Northern groups though are aware of the way in which the economic situation is going to affect women's militancy, especially at work.

Sheila Rowbotham

The idea of History Workshop at Ruskin, within the idiom of 1968, was to combine democratically people's experience and their work as working-class students at Ruskin. It was a sort of libertarian extension of the Labour History Society which communist and labour historians had formed for the older generation. I gave my first talk in public at the 1968 History Workshop. It was on the personal observations of late nineteenth-century, early twentieth-century working-class men, about their lives and feelings, men who were becoming socialists, and wrote their biographies. My talk was based on my Ph.D. Thesis, which was about working-class adult students, mainly men, and traced conflicting feelings about class and education.

At the 1968 Ruskin History Workshop a woman spoke about factory girls. A trade-union man got up and said, 'The trade-union movement is to prevent women having these terrible conditions. What we want is for women to be able to stay at home and not have to go out to work.' I got up and contested that, saying I could understand the feelings of opposition to exploitation, but at the same time it had been very important for women to earn an independent wage, and that this protective attitude was wrong and the point was to improve conditions of working women. Well, this was met with patronising laughter. I think it was from that response we got the idea of having a meeting of women. I can remember jumping up in one of the plenaries and announcing that we were going to have a meeting about women, at which point all these trade-union men laughed. The women were furious. A few of us met in a tiny student's bedroom, and we decided to call the conference. It was in keeping with a very open atmosphere at the time, with people having meetings on everything under the sun. Also, the National Joint Action Committee for Women's Equal Rights had been formed in the summer of 1968 after the Ford's Equal Pay strike. That was important for the idea of women studying their own experiences.

I came from an extremely right-wing Tory background. My father was an engineering salesman in Leeds, who did fairly well, in a lower-middle class way. It wasn't an educated background – my education was a bit of a fluke.

Until I was seven I'd lived in an area which was becoming increasingly working class and black. I lived this rather happy existence, organising gangs, fighting, being incredibly tough. When we moved, my father, unbeknown to me, actually stopped all my friends who, with their snotty noses, trailed up to visit me. I was totally isolated. People there wouldn't let their kids play with me because they said I was common.

Then when I was ten, because I had bad catarrh, I was sent off to this Methodist boarding school by the sea, which was another wrench. I became very introspective and rather sad, and lonely. When I was about thirteen I went to the cinema with this girl, and she said the Teds were 'common', and I thought 'They're alright!' They were people I liked! I think I had this emotional childhood affection about people who were despised.

The history teacher had an enormous influence on me. She was a liberal, who made me contest aspects of politics and really pushed me into trying for Oxford, which was fairly unusual. There was only one person in our school who had got in. Although our school was private, it wasn't very posh; it was geared to producing Methodist ministers' daughters, East Yorkshire farmers' wives. They emphasised religion and sport. I was hopeless at sport but quite interested in religion, particularly in theology and the history of heresies. I was a rather funny, swotty, little girl. I can remember I was let into the library when I was eleven to write an essay on St Stephen, the martyr who died from stoning. I read a book by Ronald Knox called *Enthusiasm*, and a lot of Wesley's journals, which were all about enthusiasm.

I stopped believing in God when I was about sixteen. I was influenced by the Polish father of a friend who had fought in the Resistance, had heard Juliet Greco singing in Paris, and knew about the existentialists. He was Jewish and rejected faith. I was rather shocked at somebody saying they didn't believe in God, but got really interested. Then I read Bertrand Russell and I decided I didn't really accept Christianity, but I went on being interested in spiritual being. We got 'High' Methodism at school, which was very tolerant, towards the low churches at least, wanting to have church unity, and very interested in education. By the fifties Methodism had developed a strong social conscience. There were connections to the peace movement too. I had this rather passionate encounter with a guy I met at a Methodist sixth-form college, who was part of an evangelical church, and who took me singing hymns outside pubs. It was very funny, because it was absolutely classic that the evangelical zeal was very much bound up with sexual passion. Also in Methodism there is the circle which witnesses – so that every individual discusses their own struggles and sins. There was a sense of release and a sense that the group takes some responsibility for one's own dilemmas. And there was a sexual effect in Methodism; these youth witnessing sessions always seemed to be followed by people getting off with each other, leading to union – except I was no good about contraceptives, so I stopped before total union! So did the boys, actually, they were all terrified – this was still late fifties. I was about sixteen or seventeen.

I went to Paris in 1960 – when there was a French conflict with Algeria. I was intuitively sympathetic to the Algerians without understanding it as politics. I just felt an antagonism to the French police and I'd read about torture of Algerians and so on. I went to Oxford in 1961, when I was just eighteen, and read History.

I first met Bob in the summer of 1962, when I was nineteen. I was sort of rebellious, so it wasn't such an enormous step to connect that with socialism. Before that I think I felt I couldn't really identify with workers because I didn't feel connected personally to working-class people. I remember having an argument with a man at Oxford who claimed socialism was absolutely nothing to do with personal feelings. I couldn't accept that, perhaps because of my Methodist background. Methodism did talk about your feelings. It was Bob, with his great rational knowledge of contraception, who introduced me to the diaphragm.

We came to London in 1964, and I started a Ph.D. on working-class education at Chelsea College of Advanced Technology, where I was also teaching liberal studies part-time to science students. We went to live in Hackney (because Bob had to be near Liverpool Street in order to get to Cambridge, where he was teaching). We went on this funny train, and I thought, my God, we're going to the back of beyond. We got to what seemed a rather deserted part of London. You had to walk miles to the nearest fish and chip shop. We didn't have a telephone, so people used to drop by and they would have to sit outside hopelessly.

My mother was ill, and down in London seeing a doctor. When I was visiting her at the Cumberland Hotel one day, I suddenly heard this enormous noise outside; there was a demonstration going by. There were all these young people with big pictures of Marx and Engels. I said, 'Oh, there's a

31

demonstration, I've got to go, I'll be back in a minute.' I ran out of the Cumberland Hotel in my high heels and tight skirt; the demonstration was mainly boys from the north and north-east, in leather jackets and jeans, and I was a great hit because I was all dolled up. I remember one boy had this extraordinary banner which said 'Girls Wanted, Cockers Only' and the other side said 'Up The Revolution'. It was a demonstration by the breakaway Socialist Labour League, young socialists, who had just been kicked out of the Labour Party. I didn't understand these disputes and joined the Labour Party. I drifted out of the Labour Party Young Socialists in 1967 with flower power and acid.

I used to spend an awful lot of time in the sixties arguing with young male hippies about socialism, and feeling uncomfortable with socialists because they weren't interested in hippy things. I was constantly being told off for my middle-class habits. They disapproved of my appearance because I had long straight hair and those old moth-eaten fur coats that we used to dig up, and bell-bottom trousers. These were 'trendy' clothes rather than proper working-class clothes. For younger girls there was a real sort of Mod style in East London, which I couldn't have done because I was already far too old, in my early twenties, and they were girls of sixteen who had short hair and very long leather jackets.

I was involved in the Vietnam solidarity movement from 1966. From this a group of us formed 'Agitprop' in 1968, an organisation that tried to change the ways the left communicated its propaganda, to make it more lively. Also I had connections with the May Day Manifesto grouping of older people on the left who were trying to overcome the divisions between the Communist Party and the Labour Party. They included some of the new left intellectuals of the fifties and early sixties, who were criticising the nature of work, developing a different notion of education, and looking at changes in technology. In retrospect I think their ideas are actually more interesting than the student movement of 1968, because

I think they were of long-term significance, but at the time I did not notice their significance and dismissed them as 'reformist'. I joined International Socialists (IS) early in 1968 after Enoch Powell's speech about immigration, because I felt that with the rise of racism there was a need to be part of a more organised group. I was drawn to International Socialists because they were influenced by ideas about general action and community politics, which were coming from the United States at the time; and they were more open to new forms of organising other than simply entering the Labour Party, influencing Labour Party policy and all that stuff, which was what Militant pushed. The International Socialists were more interested in people's transformations in the process of struggle. It may have appealed to me because I was in the Campaign for Nuclear Disarmament (CND) earlier, and my first experience of politics had been the direct action politics of the Committee of One Hundred. It was very important to me to see people changing. In the beginnings of the women's movement that was the most remarkable thing: seeing women changing their lives.

I met people who were starting a newspaper, *Black Dwarf*, named after an early-nineteenth century radical paper. I rather tended to see my role as a helper. I didn't think of myself as writing for it or being on the editorial board, though I had always liked writing. I'd finished my thesis by 1968 and it was three times the length it should have been; I remember going to see Eric Hobsbawm, my supervisor, who told me I should cut it. I could hear the noise of a demonstration in the street. He was telling me to cut all the rather interesting mystical people, like Edward Carpenter – he thought they were all complete rubbish. I was sympathetic to these weirdos, because they were more in tune with the idea of linking personal life and politics. I never did finish cutting my thesis. Politics took over.

Black Dwarf was started by people who were in the media world. That's what I was really attracted to, the vision and creativity. It was a terrific relief after doddering around in Hackney with all these people like Militant and IS who had the idea that the only form of communication was to 'do a leaflet' and 'speak through your loudspeaker'. There was a debate going on about women towards the end of 1968, by which time I was on the editorial board. I heard that two men had suggested that they put pin-ups in *Black Dwarf* to increase the circulation. Well, another woman opposed this on old-fashioned socialist morality grounds: socialists do not demean themselves by having pin-ups or sexy adverts, socialism is superior. Well, I didn't quite agree with this idea, but I felt uneasy, though I couldn't put it into political words. Bob got in an argument with the *New Left Review* people about strip clubs, saying that any socialist man who really believed in women's equality should be ready to go and strip outside these places in protest, but the *New Left Review* men said this was puritanical old hat.

It was agreed that one of the themes of the next issue of *Black Dwarf* should be women. One of the men was appointed to do the women's issue, because he was a proper theoretical comrade. He knew about Reich and therefore he was meant to know all about women and sex. But because I made so much noise and wouldn't shut up, I was allowed to be his helper. I had heard about the women's movement in the United States and met American radicals through their opposition to the Vietnam war. At a meeting on Vietnam in Hackney, I was amazed to see this person, who seemed like a hippy, who didn't behave like all these other guys. He gave me a lift home and said, 'The reason why they're trying to shut you up is because you're a woman.' Well, people had always told me that I talked too much, so this new explanation was a very welcome one! It was amazing to have a man saying that.

The women's issue of *Black Dwarf* came out in January 1969. I worked so hard that I completely took it over. A couple of months later I wrote a pamphlet called 'Women's

34

Liberation and the New Politics', after the *Black Dwarf* issue on women. I remember at that time friends were building a new bathroom in our house, because the floor was rotten. We had to walk on this plank to the toilet. They were busy hammering and sawing, and I felt terribly guilty not helping during the two weeks it took to write the pamphlet.

At the time I was writing I talked to Arielle Aberson, who was studying at Ruskin; she was writing about the student movement in Paris in the late 1860s. I was very interested in how people actually came to political consciousness, which I suppose is what the pamphlet was struggling to talk about. It's something that has remained a persistent interest – I still don't know the answer.

By late 1969 we were having political conflicts in *Black Dwarf* over the whole role of a socialist newspaper. I really criticised the notion of a vanguard; I thought the paper should be carrying varying socialist ideas and debates, not the line of some self-appointed clique. We had a really bitter autumn during 1969. I was working that summer at a biscuit stall in Ridley Road, and I remember dreading the meetings. But by this time the women's groups were forming and we were organising for the Ruskin conference. I left *Black Dwarf* towards the end of 1969 with relief.

When we planned the Ruskin conference, I wanted working-class women to come. They didn't, really. I recognised the need for a political conference, although my own passion was more towards understanding history. It had become evident to me when I started to write 'Women's Liberation and the New Politics', that there was a whole history which I had never learned – I read Edith Thomas's book *The Women Incendiaries* and I began to realise there was a lot more to read. I'd studied the French Revolution at university without looking at the role of women. There was so much to learn but also so many women to reach with the ideas! I can remember in 1969 I gave talks at Sheffield University, and Chesterfield Further Education College; later a whole gang of young women training there to be beauticians came down to the Oxford conference. Jean McCrindle, who was their teacher, was reminiscing to me recently, and saying these young women went on about how beautiful all the women at the Oxford conference were. It was our age, you know, we were predominantly in our twenties. But perhaps people internalise stereotypes of feminists as harridans and they were amazed we looked at all human.

The Ruskin conference was different from other conferences I'd been to because you had the amazing feeling of your whole being being completely opened, you felt totally trusting and completely as though this was your affair. Previously I'd gone in a rather external way to conferences. We were heart and soul in it, we had created it, and we loved it. I can remember the Friday, a woman with long dark hair, very young, she must have been in her early twenties, speaking with incredible passion into the microphone. There was this feeling that all these people who were really new to politics were suddenly being released to express themselves. That was very exciting.

I was so frightened before I had to speak that I literally kept rushing to the toilet. I was speaking in the Oxford Union, women weren't allowed there when I was a student, so I hadn't taken part in Union debates. It's a very different building to speak in. It's designed for the male, projecting kind of orator, not for a woman who is simply talking, so it was really hard to speak, much harder than it would have been in Ruskin, which is a friendly little hall. I had a strong feeling that it was terribly important I didn't speak badly. We were showing that women could take on bastions like the Oxford Union and change their social meaning.

I was alarmed at the eruption from the libertarian Marxist people who sprayed the slogan, 'Woman in labour keep capital in power'. I thought it was silly; I've always felt impatient with that sort of demonstrative politics, it seems to me a very individualistic thing, just defying the authorities. I

36

believed in direct action, but direct action collectively to make a point when it was strategically useful. I suppose I'd still got the real old left idea which was that politics wasn't to do with just your individual subjective expression. I've always felt friendly towards people who have had those demonstrative politics, but I also feel really that they're not mine. So I've always been a bit of a betwixt and between creature.

I don't think we thought of what we were saying as politics. I think you just thought, 'Well, I don't really like this', or 'I do agree with that'. After Ruskin we set up a central committee structure, the Women's National Co-ordinating Committee. It was mainly women in the left groups who saw the importance of a central committee, because their organisations had central committees and they knew that was how you organised things, with a programme. I thought you needed a structure, but I was far too influenced by the new left and the May Day Manifesto to accept notions of central committees uncritically. I never was a Leninist in that sense.

As a historian, I was very interested in the way the American new left influenced the emergence of women's liberation. Consciousness-raising came from the new left out of civil rights; the slogan 'The personal is political' comes from the American student movement. These were not biological intuitions of the women's movement, they were a creative inheritance from a wider political rebellion in more than one country.

I didn't want us to be co-opted by the revolutionary left groups but I didn't feel hostile to the women in International Socialists. They wanted what I wanted, which was a movement that wouldn't alienate working-class women and trade union women. However, one really interesting contradiction is that those of us who were influenced by American feminism were saying we wanted to look at our own oppression, that we were from this stratum of middle-class women who have valid reasons to complain; this was a really important

37

aspect of women's liberation politics. At the same time, though, an assumption in the socialist milieu I was in was that we wanted to extend our base and we don't want to be limited to a particular social group. The two things were equally strong, and they were quite contradictory. When you write them down, they're in conflict, but in practice for a long time we acted out both. Clearly, by talking about a women's movement we were saying that it was possible to transcend class distinctions, and implicitly other distinctions like race. Yet we knew there was a gap between our grievances and those of working-class women. Of course, nowadays this is all questioned in terms of the politics of difference, but then we were trying to create a unity, which I believe is still necessary. The argument that one organises on the basis of one's own oppression came partly from the American new left and the Black movement. This was obviously connected with social changes in the States which preceded Britain, but are happening in capitalism generally, in which there's a whole stratum of people who are not clear whether they are working class or new middle class or whatever. There is a stratum which is different from manual workers, and isn't the old owning bourgeoisie or even the upper-middle-class professional people. We were thrown up by a new social process. I think a lot of feminists came from working-class families, who had gone to university for the first time, or were from a lower-middle-class uneducated background and had been pushed up to meet upper-middle-class people by being educated, as in my own case. A lot of us were in this process of class transition.

It was both a social process and a psychological process, being cut off from our own class background, through education, and probably feeling rather guilty, in a repressed way, about that. We were in this very acute class tension, so in saying we had the right to assert our own oppression, we were saying something about this new stratum of people. We were also going back to the earlier utopian socialists and adapting for women an anarcho-syndicalist position of autonomous action. James Connolly, one of the first people that the New York radical feminists reprinted, wrote on women in 1913, and said that those who actually wore the chains were best fitted to break them. This idea has its own problem but it felt like an electrifying concept and gave us legitimacy to contest the men in the Marxist groups. At the same time, I didn't feel completely divorced from the Marxists, because I did feel that the working classes were crucial in the process of transforming society, and therefore this movement must extend itself to find a link with working-class women; I didn't know how.

We lived an amazing ambiguity, with two quite contradictory ideas, but I think that is what social movements are like. People carry around ideas which, if you stopped to consider, you would think incompatible; but actually we did have both, we were saying yes, we are going to talk about our oppression, *and* we're going to go out to working-class women.

For a time in the 1970s there were all-embracing annual women's liberation conferences. When socialist feminist conferences started to develop, they brought together those of us who felt a very strong emphasis on process, on not pushing our politics at people, seeing socialist feminism more as an approach rather than as a programme.

From Bristol (1973) I think I began to feel slightly uncomfortable at women's liberation conferences. I seemed to see a politics that was identifying feminism as something more to do with a personal way of dressing or lifestyle, and I didn't really ever like that. I always felt uneasy about the idea of divorcing yourself from women who were outside the feminist movement or the left. What had been good, to me, when the women's movement was beginning, was the fact that we wanted to reach lots of women, women who were in Housewives' Register and anywhere, church groups, Chesterfield FE College, or wherever.

At the Skegness women's liberation conference (1972) my

main feeling was hostility to the Maoists, but I also felt uneasy about the radical feminists. A group of women stormed a miners' strip show that was going on next door; I felt that wasn't the correct tactic. I think if I'd had been a bit more clear-headed, I would have argued for picketing it, because then the men would actually have had to cross the picket line and argue, whereas if you invade, they react violently and chuck you out.

When it happened a local woman at the bar was terribly upset because she'd heard this discussion at the conference attacking the family, and she couldn't understand why we were attacking the family. I got into a long discussion with her, and she decided that because I came from the north of England I could be saved from this dreadful feminist fate, and decided to try and fix me up with the barman, who she thought was a nice young lad who would sort me out. I was rather involved in this when somebody came rushing in and said, 'They're brutalising the sisters'; I didn't really understand what was going on. It was because the radical feminists had invaded the striptease. Meanwhile I was trying to campaign for women office cleaners who worked at night, and I was arguing against these Hemel Hempstead Maoists who were attacking the lesbians, and also trying to argue with the miners to convince them that they should support women's liberation after they'd all shouted all night 'Women's lib, get your knickers off'. So quite early on some of the contradictions in our politics were actually exploding about our ears. I came back from Skegness and actually got quite ill, vomiting and diarrhoea. I'm sure it was a psychosomatic thing, like an infant – no control. Things were coming out of me and I couldn't stop them.

I had my son Will in 1977. Around this time I began to get very depressed by discussions at women's liberation conferences and by articles in feminist magazines. And in the late seventies and early eighties I felt really estranged from what it seemed that the women's movement had become. I didn't agree with the politics that emphasised male violence and saw pornography as an extension of rape, indistinguishable from the actual physical violation of women. Women's liberation no longer seemed like a revelation, it was part of wider political arguments.

By the mid-seventies many women without any Marxist or political background had been drawn into the movement. They had a sort of American religious revivalist inspiration. They were not weighed down by old dictums, but they also disregarded the mistakes of the past. Their faith and enthusiasm for participatory democracy landed us, I think, with some of the problems that the Greeks had – when people disagree the only thing you can do is to ostracise – in Ancient Greece somebody would be sent outside the city. And that was the problem in this politics; if somebody disagreed and the consensus developed against that person or minority, then there could only be ejection. It was an ill wind that blew nobody any good. It meant that we had a proliferation of different groups appearing in many aspects of life, and entering areas of life where orthodox socialist politics were far too slow. But in the long run it meant disagreements were simply left hanging rather than resolved.

My response was like a lot of women, to ease out of the women's groups and go into more general socialist politics. When Lynne Segal and Hilary Wainwright and I wrote a pamphlet called 'Beyond the Fragments' (Merlin 1979) it was to try to ensure that the experience of an autonomous movement contributed to a better socialist movement. In the late seventies it did seem that there were changes in the Labour Party, and that seemed to be the place to try to bring some of these understandings of the seventies into politics. It proved rather more complicated in practice than many of us could envisage at the time.

I never had a notion of a career, in the typical sixties complacent way; I just thought you lived for politics and earned enough money to survive. I'd laboured through this

41

enormous thesis but I hadn't thought about women in history. The women's movement changed that. I had this overwhelming sense of having to write about everything because of the times, this feeling that nobody had ever done anything before and everything had to be said anew; that you had to create the whole of culture.

Raya Levin

I was born in Russia. I went to school in Switzerland, Austria and Palestine, university in Heidelberg and Paris, and came to England at the end of 1936, after having studied, qualified and then worked in France for over six years. I had already been a communist from my mid-teens. My family were a very politicised family, but more in the direction of Zionism. I became a communist as a sort of opposition to Zionism, considering that the Jewish problem, (very much like the women's problem later on), would be solved by socialists. Going down the nationalist road would only bring about a reactionary solution to the Jewish problem. I didn't sense discrimination or oppression, either as a Jew or as a woman, because I was supported by like-minded people.

I arrived in England married. In 1936 I worked for an ordinary solicitor. I was a foreign lawyer working in an international firm of solicitors specialising in foreign law, I spoke English, French and German, so was in the international department. Then the war broke out and they gave me my articles, and I qualified.

I worked for many years in private practice, and also worked as a legal adviser to the Holloway Prison Aid Society, in the 1950s. The Society was taken over by the probation service, so I transferred to the probation service; because of

43

my legal training they allocated me special work with prisoners who had legal problems in civil life, divorce, rent
arrears, hire purchase agreements or bankruptcy – anything
like that. In 1970 I was specially attached to the after-care
unit, in Southwark; part of my work there was to visit
prisoners prior to their discharge and help with arrangements
for their release, employment, accommodation, medical
treatment and so on.

I was very aware early on of the complex position of the
Soviet Union with respect to communism. Yet my confidence
in communism as such was never shaken. It was the only
alternative to fascism. In Yugoslavia, all right, communism
could go a different way, it was a Soviet Union failure, not
necessarily the failure of communism. Then there was China.
For a long time I was very heartened by China. Then there
was Cuba. Really it wasn't until the late 1970s that I began to
realise there didn't seem to be any real movement in my
lifetime which would materialize into anything which I could
identify with.

I don't consider myself belonging to any particular country
because of my background. I feel you could drop me in a
parachute anywhere in the globe and I'd get adapted. A bit
more difficult now than twenty years ago. So I never looked
at communists as a British party, or a French party. It seemed
to me to reflect the global situation.

I'm not a member of the Communist Party any more. I just
faded out. Metal fatigue! I identified with CND in the 1950s
and so on. I must say that the women's movement really
began to mean something to me – the problem of women as
distinct from the problems of socialism – when I worked in
Holloway. It was an absolute eye-opener. It was the first time
I was in very close contact with women all of whom were
working class – particularly disadvantaged working class.
Then I saw that their problems had to be separate, on a
different level altogether. I felt that one should try and press
the Communist Party, but I didn't feel that any party would
take up women's issues satisfactorily; women had to do it

44

themselves. I could see that the problems which I recognised in women in Holloway existed for women everywhere, although they were very much disguised.

This is where I was constantly protected – I was very well qualified. Professionally I was treated as an equal, paid as an equal: I was in a minority. I heard recently that in the Soviet Union 70 per cent of the doctors are women, and that the profession as such has declined in status because of that. I was a special case; I wasn't a threat to anybody.

In 1970, just before Ruskin, I had been given a Fellowship at the Institute of Criminology in Cambridge, and I was visiting a number of prisons all over the country. I was given a grant for nine months, seconded from the probation service, to write up about twenty cases I had on long-term prisoners, mainly men. At the beginning, especially in places like Holloway, I found the work a bit alarming. But I was really surprised at the close relationship one could form in a very short time. Time is quite different in prison – if you go and visit somebody for half an hour, it is like having spent a holiday with them. They are so concerned in their expectations of the visit, so it's very much more intense than other relationships. The people I was in contact with were on license on release, so they had to keep in touch with me for a time. It was entirely our decision as to how frequently we kept in touch, and in what manner, either by writing or by visiting, or by telephone. Quite often when they got into minor trouble during that period, I would really put all my legal wiliness into getting them a non-custodial sentence.

My main aim was that they should not go back to prison. Prison is a self-perpetuating thing. I've found – and this was the subject of my work in Cambridge – that the longer they were out of prison the more capable they were of functioning. I was dealing with a whole range of people and most had very long sentences, but not because they'd committed very heinous crimes. Every time the sentence got longer and longer. That is why I felt that if they stayed out of prison for two years, they were virtually sure to be able to manage. These were mainly people who were convicted of crimes against property. Housebreaking, or robbery – they were called different things at different times – but it was usually done without violence, to empty houses. I never got too indignant at all about crimes against property. Crimes against the person bother me very much. I haven't worked out exactly how I ought to deal with people who are violent towards or injure others. I've thought a great deal, but I can't pretend to have an answer to it. But crimes against property I personally, emotionally, treat very lightly, so I never felt very judgemental.

In the late sixties I was involved also with the new left. That was a very turbulent time for me really, because there were so many crossroads. There was the CND, there was the women's movement. There was a question of free thinking, what is a party, is a party necessary. And of course there was my niece, Arielle Aberson, who was at Ruskin; she broke away from her home and came here, she was kicking against Switzerland. My main preoccupation at the time was, can one help the revolution forward without the frame of a party? The party seemed to me not to be functioning in any shape or form. I would discuss it with a circle of friends. A lot of ex-communists, who left in 1968, and some quite a lot earlier. It was not in any organised kind of way, but we'd chip in if anything was going that seemed to raise issues.

I was involved with a woman's group perhaps shortly before Ruskin. But you see, consciousness-raising groups were not for me; I felt none of these problems applied to me. I was not confined, I was not denied development. I had seen it in Holloway or wherever, but it didn't apply to me.

I heard about Ruskin from Arielle, and I became part of the organising committee. I think it was very spontaneous; none of us had any idea that it would escalate into such proportions. People at Ruskin were willing to lend us their meeting room, and we thought perhaps fifteen to twenty people would come – a hundred people would have been considered a great success – we meant to hold it in Ruskin itself. But then the applications just poured in. At the time Arielle was staying with me, we were staggered by the number of applications. Then about a month or a fortnight before we had to book a big hall, the Union hall. Some people were staying in Ruskin, the creche was in Ruskin, and the smaller groups were in Ruskin. But the actual conference was in the Union hall.

There were over five hundred women. We were absolutely flabbergasted. Who's going to speak, who's going to put resolutions . . .? People wanted to express various things. And everybody could put down a resolution. There was somewhere where they just handed in what they wanted to say. The only thing the organising committee did was organise a few papers.

There were all sorts of left-wing groupings – Trotskyists, Maoists. In the beginning it was all very informal, trying to size up the extent of it, and finding out what people wanted to talk about. I think we must have met about a dozen times. There were lots of leaflets and questionnaires that had to be printed – it's all coming back to me now. They were sent to different people, what did they want to discuss, how many people could they send. Seeing how we could accommodate all these various needs that were expressed. There were a large number of women's groups who wrote in, student groups from universities. In spite of the fact that we tried to get away from left-wing parties, the parties took a great deal of interest in it. I hoped that it wouldn't resort to a squabble because the various parties were saying, 'We are the champions of women.' But it wasn't like that. I chaired a small discussion group on delinquency, connected with a paper I wrote.

I went up to Ruskin on the Friday. It was pandemonium. The whole thing had such an air of excitement; anything could happen, it was so unexpected. We didn't know until

47

the last minute who would or wouldn't come, who would speak and who wouldn't speak.

I remember a lot of hassle about the creche, because there were many more children than expected. The Ruskin male students had offered to run the creche, and they did, but it got a bit beyond them. A few women had to rush backwards and forwards during the conference, because the men weren't used to it. I think there was a fair amount of agreement in the organising committee that men should be excluded, and then at the conference itself it was felt that there were certain areas one could let men in, because it had overflowed to such a degree. I think people felt that men should perhaps listen – there was a bit of argument – I thought it should be women only. Men could contribute later if they wanted to in ancillary capacities, but the actual direction of the movement, the aims of the movement, should be determined by women, otherwise we were back in the old parties.

I thought it was a breakthrough. I was very euphoric, after almost ten years in the doldrums. All the other things were very bitty. Vietnam wasn't us, Czechoslovakia wasn't us, Paris wasn't us. This was a major movement which shook up Britain, there's no question about it. As a conference it was extremely refreshing. People were talking in a very spontaneous way without any bureaucracy, no standing orders committee, resolution B and amendment C, all this kind of thing, and really very little formal decision, very little voting. In fact, I don't think there was any voting – perhaps at the end about forming some permanent body. It fitted in with my idea that politics in the future must go much more in interest groups than in parties. Young people for the demands of youth, and women for the demands of women, and racial minorities for their rights. Transcending party politics. I was very aware of the fact that we were still very much marginal to women workers, to my Holloway women as I saw them, but I thought the impetus seemed to be so unpolitical. And because it was unpolitical and appealed to

48

women's own concerns, I hoped it would penetrate to the working-class women. It didn't worry about parliament, it didn't worry about getting political power in the structure of society as all other parties were. It was a bit anarchic really, in feeling. It would be something, not quite like a trade-union movement, a movement of women determined to get their share and their due in society. I wasn't seeing it in any rigid structural formation, but just a groundswell of women.

I felt a lot of personal elements in my life hadn't been explored because I was protected. I was never tied to a kitchen sink. Nevertheless, I suddenly realised I was tied in other ways which I wasn't aware of. I solved it in a very middle-class way by having domestic help, so that I could work professionally, and my children would be looked after. But then I realised that I was responsible for it all. In addition to the worry of my work, I had to carry the organising load of the household on my shoulders. It had never struck me that it was an extra burden.

It was also very interesting to discover all sorts of ways in which I quite unconsciously used my femininity to get the better of my male colleagues. You think there was no discrimination, but sometimes there was positive discrimination in my favour. I felt very often that the women in Holloway were a particularly disadvantaged group – because they were not even able to use that little bit of extra edge. I've always thought there were a very small number of women delinquents, comparatively, due to the fact that women have this upward mobility, which men haven't got; they can lift themselves out of their situation through their sexual behaviour. Whereas if a man wants to get upwardly mobile fairly quickly and hasn't the circumstances, he has no choice except to resort to lawbreaking. A middle-class man is much more likely to marry an attractive working-class girl than the other way round.

At Ruskin it was wonderful to see so many vivacious and outspoken women, women with so many ideas. My feeling

49

was that there was now a generation coming who were going to replace party politics by something very much more stimulating and much more fruitful, not so stultifying. I identified with it, but I never thought I would take part in it; it was another generation.

I didn't like the graffiti such as 'Down with Penis Envy' because I thought they entirely barked up the wrong tree, giving ammunition to people who said that was what women's problem really was, whereas I saw it just as envy of a privileged position of man in society (if there was any envy at all). I felt it was very nasty; Ruskin were the hosts. I had to intervene with the dean of the college, partly because of my age, partly because I was a solicitor, because he wanted to take steps against people. I had to talk with him and said it would be cleaned up. They didn't call the police; I poured oil on troubled waters, and we started cleaning it up before it became a public scandal. All the chaps who helped with the creche and so on – they thought it was very nasty towards them. What worried me was the feeling behind it. If they wanted to do it they should have gone and defaced some police station. Why deface Ruskin College?

Arielle died very soon after that. In a car accident. Ruskin was in February, and she was killed on 19th April. I was terribly shattered. For a time I lost track of what went on. Then I went for a period of Fellowship at Cambridge. I lived in Madingley Hall, it was marvellous, wonderful; not having anything to do except think about what I wanted to think about, and everybody so helpful. Then I returned to my job, and I worked there till I retired in 1977, when I reached the age of sixty five. Then I worked part time several years in law centres in Notting Hill Gate and Paddington.

In the 1970s I read a lot, all the books that came out about the women's movement. Everything. I became increasingly disappointed at the way the movement was going – it really failed to influence or to create a culture of its own. I don't know how to put it; everybody accepts that human beings have got what are described as feminine qualities and masculine qualities, we all have some of each, and they're being polarized by conditioning and so on. But it seemed to me that the women's struggle was taking a competitive form. Women were feeling more and more that in order to be successful they'd got to act like men. Professionally, and in every other way. For instance, this insistence that women should go into the police, or go into the army, which were institutions I wanted abolished. There was definitely a push that women wanted to be equal, and therefore they wanted to penetrate every kind of male stronghold, and they could only penetrate them by adopting male characteristics.

Not only that, in the business world for instance, instead of forming new types of co-operative businesses, or something that would challenge the male-dominated culture, they adapted to the male-dominated culture. I mean, there's no question they made strides forward in terms of achieving greater equality, there's greater penetration in the professions. But I felt it was all the time at the cost of abandoning what women could really contribute to society, in the way of looking at things differently, of negating certain structures altogether, of challenging the structure. The more libertarian and radical feminist parts of the women's movement seemed to me to be eventually captured by the lesbians. You couldn't have a mass movement on the basis of lesbianism.

Another thing I felt – I know it's very unpractical and there's no way one could achieve it under capitalism – but I felt that women going to work is an economic necessity, and there are more and more driven into the badly paid jobs, so that equal pay doesn't mean anything. More than anything else, I felt that women should have a choice whether they wanted to look after children or not. They shouldn't be told that they can't look after children fulltime and be feminist. I feel that very strongly. It's always looked on from the professional woman's point of view – she can do an interesting job. But for somebody who goes washing up at a cafeteria in British Rail or cleaning offices, to look after her children is far less dull. She only goes and does it because she needs the money, and if she had the money she could decide if she wanted to go to work or not.

I felt by the mid- or late-seventies terribly fragmented. I had experienced so much fragmentation in politics, I couldn't go the same road under feminism. I retreated more and more into just reading – I'm always interested in everything that's going on, and on a personal level I would discuss and so on. But I felt, 'I've served my time'. It's just a question of really keeping abreast of developments and knowing what's going on. I still believe in soviets and believe in grass-roots participation, but I don't believe, and never have, that we can capture the state in a parliamentary way. It's a fallacy to think one can change a state by votes. In order for women to penetrate into the position of power they have to adapt themselves to the structure. And that's what they've done, and that's why they've lost a lot of what made it tremendously exciting in the beginning. I don't pretend I have the solution to the problem. But it definitely is a problem. Any kind of movement that allows itself to be channelled into existing structures I feel is doomed to failure. There seems to be so far no mechanism whereby revolutionary fervour can be kept alive and made effective without being channelled and made into a rigid power structure.

The women's movement has made an impact, in a way one could say very similar to the Russian Revolution. It showed that if people really do feel strongly about what they want to achieve and are willing to go outside existing structures, then it is very inspiring.

There are certain things that are not accepted any more in relation to the oppression of women. Certain kinds of expression of sexism are no longer possible or permissible – not socially acceptable – that the women's movement has achieved. I think there has been little impact on men in general; superficially, men have realised there are certain things they can't permit themselves any longer. But there is still basically the main culture intact.

Feminine values to me are the values which come in conflict with a patriarchal hierarchical class structure. Like ambition in achieving status. I see them as male values. The counterpart would be co-operation, working with other people. That is what I really feel women could contribute to human society, and have been prevented from doing, because of the competitiveness which has dominated society for the past several hundred years. To achieve equality with men in the present structure means to adopt their values. You enter a man's world. If you want to compete with them, there's no way they'll let you compete unless it's on their terms.

We're talking about professional women, business women, media women. For working-class women, their feminism depends basically on them having a choice between working in terms which are acceptable to them, and being mothers without being dependent on men. This is what I felt so much at Holloway. What they needed was financial independence. They said they couldn't put up with having to coax the man round to getting a new coat – the humiliation – they would rather pinch it. They were not conformist women, they could bring it out much more openly. They didn't want to have to sweeten him up in order to get what they wanted. One could put it in a very simplistic way by saying that mothers should get a wage for looking after children and everybody else should contribute to a fund; all males and all female non-parents, i.e. all non-mothers, should contribute to this fund. Looking after children, bringing up children – women who want to do it – it should be open to them. Some or even many may not want to do it. But if they want to do it they should not have to fall back on individual men.

Now, how you work it out I don't know. But it is an absolutely crucial requirement, because during childbearing years women do have to depend on somebody or something in any society, and they should not be tied to any specific man in order to get that support. I think if that knot were cut, then one could really see an upsurge of women coming into their own.

I don't know what I am by now, Russian, or Jewish, or French or whatever. I've been 'British', in quotes, for over fifty years, but never felt British. I'm what the Communists used to call 'a rotten cosmopolitan'. There was a period when the Soviet Union was very dependent on the nationalistic feeling of its people before the war and during the war. They were very opposed to anything cosmopolitan, they regarded it as rotten. I'm very comfortable being a rotten cosmopolitan.

Anna Davin

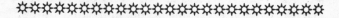

At History Workshop 4 at Ruskin in November 1969, at the end of the morning session, which was on Victorian London, Sheila Rowbotham stood up and said that she was working specifically on women's history, and was anyone else? She gave out a time and place for anyone interested to meet, but before she could get to that practical point there was a great guffaw from the floor. Ruskin is a trade-union college, and in 1969 it was male-dominated and had some very traditional men. Clearly it seemed funny to them that women's history could be seen as needing separate attention, or that there'd be any point in our getting together. Sheila made her call in spite of the guffaw, and the meeting happened, but we had been horrified at that reaction. I was totally furious, and at the next possible opportunity, I think as the next session began, I remember standing up, knees knocking, to voice my indignation and explain why it was politically improper for people to have that reaction, and why anyone who thought of themselves as on the left and pioneering social history would have to change their tune. I said that the men who'd laughed should be ashamed of themselves. Afterwards a number of Ruskin students came and said they were ashamed of having laughed, or disassociated themselves from those who had.

55

I'd just finished a history degree at Warwick, and was living in Coventry but coming to Oxford fairly often, because my parents lived there and because I was getting a lot of support from R., who taught at Ruskin, in following through a research project. I was taking a year off, which as a (then) married woman I was able to do; and as I'd pushed myself hard as a student and had had TB in the middle without taking time to make up, I felt justified. I had three children, ten, eight and six, at this point. I was twenty six when I started at university; twenty nine at the Ruskin conference. I'd grown up in Oxford, not as part of the left but with a lot of cultural and intellectual stimulus from my parents and their friends, and the assumptions I grew up with were basically liberal – women were as good as men, and racism was bad. At about sixteen I got to know L. through a cousin in his household being in my class at school. Out of that grew courtship and our marriage, in 1958, when I was eighteen. L.'s family were left wing, and so was he. I got more interested in politics, and started going to political meetings and listening to political talk. In these years, when *New Left Review* was emerging out of *New Reasoner* and *Universities and Left Review*, we had friends in both groupings, though we saw more of the new generation. So in my late teens and early twenties a lot of political discussion was going on, around feminist issues too at times; we read De Beauvoir's *Second Sex*, and Juliet Mitchell lived with us one year. But I was a kind of looker-on at student life, full of envy for the time they all had to read and think, and have affairs with each other.

I was younger than all of them, and my time was consumed with having three children in four years and running a house. L. did most of the cooking and shared other work, but he somehow also did his maths, but I was a bit of a mother-figure, and our house was somewhere friends came to talk and relax, and sometimes to bring problems.

My parents both had their secondary and university education through scholarships, and they were each in the first generation of their Irish-New Zealand families to do that. They expected me and my sisters to want the same, but we didn't have the same obstacles or ambitions or understanding, and instead I suppose we all dodged off. My two sisters and I all left school prematurely; my mother kept having to write 'Dear Miss S., My daughter has decided to leave school and get married.' I thought university was going to be like more school, and I wasn't interested at that point. I was pregnant at eighteen; my mother was distressed but also supportive. She said she liked L., but I was very young, and we should consider an abortion. (Of course this was before the 1967 Act made that easier.) I said, 'No, no, I love him,' and we got married. I did get a cap after Dom was born (1959), but I wasn't terrible consistent about using it. Kathy was born two years later, and Mick before another two years. So I was pretty busy. And although I was in love, and loved the children, I did come to agree with my mother that marriage was rather a major step to take so young. I hated not having my own name, too.

After the first years in Oxford we had a year in the United States, and then a year when L. taught at Algiers University, which wasn't an easy one for me as I knew almost nobody and hated men's behaviour to me in the street. We went back to England in June 1965, for L. to start teaching at the new University of Warwick. That summer I learnt to drive and we bought a car. It was also the summer I first hitch-hiked, with one of three friends whose free behaviour I envied. They were a woman and two men, part of a set who hitched everywhere singly or together, who didn't seem to care what they were wearing or when they would eat or where sleep, who just enjoyed life by the minute and were great fun to be with whenever they turned up. By then, in the mid-sixties, I was restless and knew I'd had enough of being only a housewife. I applied for a place at Warwick, to study history, because E. P. Thompson was teaching there and I liked his recent book *The Making of the English Working Class*. Then I got cold feet – I hadn't written an essay or done any disciplined reading for eight years. But L. and family and friends encouraged me, and Dorothy Thompson set me an essay, then read it and said it was fine. Then I nearly lost the chance by getting pregnant again, but women friends helped organize an abortion, and after that I went on the pill.

I loved being a student, and of course the late 1960s were heady years. As in Oxford, we kept open house for my new student friends, as well as old friends who came for weekends. I threw myself into everything – folk club and film club, politics, study too. We had a series of Yugoslav au pair girls, which with the full share in parenting which L. always took, made it possible. –

In 1969 some of us from the Socialist Society started a women's liberation group. We were probably partly influenced by American visitors (the History Department had an exchange scheme where we got forty American students a year), some of whom were in SDS (Students for a Democratic Society) and brought feminist pamphlets and ideas. And we ran a bookstall which included pamphlets sent from the New England Press.

I had a rather sexy self-image in the late sixties I think. The photographs show me in mini-skirts, sometimes black fishnet tights. I enjoyed showing myself off. I started having affairs, and taking the initiative – as I was a married woman and older I probably had to make it more obvious that I was interested. It was part of my wanting to join in student life. I was sowing the wild oats I hadn't sown earlier on. 1965 to 1970 for me was very definitely a breaking out period, and dressing that way went with that. Later, in the 1970s, I went back to trousers, with plain blue cotton jackets – maybe Chinese influence via my sister, (who after two years living in China and three doing her first degree was now writing a thesis on women in China). I never wore dungarees: they

58

seemed like a fashion within the women's movement and I resisted them.

In 1967 I started a passionate affair with an Italian man. We'd met during the year in the US, and he came to visit. The attraction was very powerful, and I was being hard-line about my independence. I told L. I'd always said I wasn't comfortable with monogamy, and if he loved me he wouldn't mind! I made all sorts of pseudo-political, self-deceiving, unrealistic rationalisations to justify myself, which I now feel very stern and disapproving about. That affair then went on rather powerfully for the next eighteen months, through the period when I had TB. B. was always in Italy or Switzerland so we never had long together, though I spent three weeks with him when convalescent. Then in August 1968 we were in a summer hut in the Alps, very primitive but beautiful. The Russians invaded Czechoslovakia: we were listening to the radio all the time and arguing – I was indignant, and he was defending them. It poured with rain all the time. I hadn't any Swiss money, because I'd forgotten to change my pounds before he whisked me away from the airport. We were twenty minutes walk from the last point the car could get to, and that was a village which had a bus once a week. So I couldn't walk out. It was all a bit awful. He had that European communist style of very hard discussion. He wanted me to be able to have arguments with him on things where he already had a line and I didn't, but he knew I didn't agree. So I found him intellectually quite threatening, and politically too confident. The passion was still there, but I couldn't stand the arguments, and afterwards we stopped seeing each other. Along with my frenetic student life and growing desire for independence, that affair was part of why L. and I were to break up in 1970.

After my finals in 1969, I went on with a research project of my own, reading books and microfilm in the Warwick library, and enjoying student life without having to meet its obligations. I went over to Oxford for the History Workshops, and also on a delegation when students were occupying the Clarendon Building, and for a meeting at Ruskin on student issues. After Sheila's call at the 1969 History Workshop, those of us who came together decided to have a workshop specifically on women's history, and to hold it at Ruskin. It was a way of showing that historical work on women could be done, was being done, that more should be done, and also to give support to those who were doing it, or wanted to. We set up a planning group which I suppose I was on – I'm rather vague about this. What I remember is that it stopped being a history conference rather quickly, and I felt some resentment, because it was a time in which doing women's history was difficult – we were always being told there would be no source material, for instance. I thought we needed to get together for support and for exchange of ideas and information. I felt the conference had been hijacked.

There was a decision not to have men in the workshops, but to allow them to come to the plenary sessions. I know what my line would have been, probably. A leaflet from our Warwick women's group, in my handwriting, says 'Women's Liberation, People's Liberation' all round the margins. At Warwick we had a mixed group at first, then stopped so as to exclude particular men who had been dominating the discussions. But I would have argued, did argue, that you couldn't change society without changing everybody's consciousness. So women needed to organise separately and have discussions on our own, but men couldn't be totally excluded; there had to be some communication between the – as it were – converted and consciousness-raised women and the unregenerate men, or nothing could really go forward. Workshops for women only with mixed plenaries would be a logical development from that, and men could organise their own workshops if they got it together.

I chaired at least one session, a plenary – I might have chaired two. The conference became a very important step in feminist organisation in Britain, and I was conscious of that at the time. I was excited by that. That doesn't mean to say that the historian in me was quieted, because I see historical understanding as essential to feminism anyway. I saw my historical research as a political activity, always. I got used to having to defend that. In 1970 L. and I moved to London. I lived with R. and he with J. The children spent part of the week in each household. I was pretty active in the early seventies. I went to a lot of meetings and demonstrations. I did a day a week in the Women's Liberation Workshop office in Little Newport Street. I was starting research on women in late-nineteenth century London, for the Ph.D. I'd registered for.

I was getting to know London. It was an angry, difficult time. We were setting up the divorce and working out what to do about the children. Awful. I remember the solicitor spent hours trying to convince me to claim all rights over them, and I was saying no, that was absolutely not fair, we'd completely shared bringing up the children and cared equally about them, and even though we were on bad terms we'd get over it. It no doubt made the divorce more expensive, having to argue with him.

I started going to the Women's History Group in the summer of 1970. It was mainly a study group. I already knew some of the women, but I was very daunted by it. I often didn't know the books they were talking about, and I was disappointed that it wasn't more historical – they were discussing psychoanalysis. I was immersing myself in late-nineteenth century London. I was rather scared of consciousness-raising groups. At Warwick I think we avoided that kind of discussion by being ultra-political, activist and socialist. In London the avoidance was less acceptable to me. I felt uneasy at not being or having been in a consciousness-raising group, and I made excuses to myself. To other people I suspect I was less honest. I think to other people I was saying, 'Well, of course the Warwick group was partly about

61

that, we discussed all those kinds of things, we knew each other.' But we hadn't, or not enough. Later I joined the Stratford women's liberation group, which balanced between a study group and 'consciousness-raising'. And all through these years I was developing close friendships, so some of that self-examination and discussion was happening outside any group.

At the same time I was getting into my historical research. I needed a recuperation from the excitement of five years of break-out. I needed to re-establish myself as somebody solid. I'd learnt that I could hold my own intellectually and politically and sexually, and now I needed to consolidate. It was hard to combine research with being an activist, and I wrote an article which defended spending my time on history. In 1973 I became involved with the new Hackney People's Autobiography Group, tape-recording local people and trying to involve them in writing their own history. For me this was about giving women a voice and a place in history. It was a new way of combining my politics and history, better than simply making women the subject of my research. There were also History Workshop activities, like the workshop conferences which I helped to organise, and spoke at, whose subjects in 1972–3 included 'Childhood', 'Women in History', and 'Family, Work and Home'. From 1972 we produced thirteen pamphlets. Ruskin students wrote them, R. edited them. I would prepare the text for the typist, then for the printers, and help with publicity and distribution. Then we started a series of History Workshop books, and I was very closely involved with the first couple; then *History Workshop Journal*, whose editorial collective I still work on.

After a visit to my sister in Paris, in 1972, I joined a self-defence group back in London. She and I had got into a scuffle with a man who was hassling us as we walked home one night; although we'd routed him I'd felt annoyed both at having lost my temper and at being relatively ineffective in a fight. So when I heard that an informal and mixed self-defence group was being started by comrades at the School of Oriental and African Studies, I went along. To start with it was fairly evenly men and women. But the women were quite a strong bunch, and started to challenge the teacher's language and teaching style as authoritarian and sexist. W. accepted the criticisms, and improved. I thought he was changing his whole being, not just his manner, in the course of that. I think I was wrong, or I expected too much. But I wanted to believe people could change, and it attracted me to him, along with his capacity to make us laugh, and his intelligence, though it was several years before we got together properly. Women came to dominate the self-defence group. It lasted about four years, till 1976 or 1977. It was certainly part of my being a feminist. I felt generally more confident, and I discovered that I loved fighting. My favourite part of the class was at the end, when we paired off and fought. It needed stamina, which I didn't have: I never put in enough solid practice. But my natural balance and quick eye were useful, and sometimes I was good at outguessing the other person; and it was a completely licensed outlet for being aggressive – a need I'd never allowed myself to admit to. And it was very physical. We never had proper changing rooms. We simply undressed and dressed again at the side of the room without bothering about being men and women. I liked that.

I was also in a group called 'Women Against Population Control' around 1973. It stimulated my article on 'Imperialism and Motherhood' (*History Workshop Journal* 5, Spring 1978). We were campaigning for wider access to abortion, but we stressed that choice should be available either way – that abortion should be available on demand, but that women should also be free to bear children as and when they wanted. We pointed out how states want to control fertility for their own economic and political ends, and how this produces pressure or coercion on women, some or all. We produced one leaflet, I think. I was simultaneously finding out about the origins of welfare clinics in the infant health movement of the 1890s and 1900s, and the connection with anxieties about 'national efficiency'. I was thinking how many of those babies whose lives were first saved grew up to be cannon fodder in World War I, or to bear children who grew up in time for World War II. It made me think about state policies in relation to women, children and the family.

In 1975 I went to live with W., and in 1977 had a child with him – my fourth and last. Motherhood this time was harder. With the first ones, that was what I wanted to be doing, even though I felt jealous of everyone else's freedom. This time, I knew I wanted to be writing. I was finishing off 'Imperialism and Motherhood' towards the end of the pregnancy and when Sally was first born. I was very depressed for some months, which I thought was because I had to wean her after a breast abscess, but was probably about the frustration of not managing to write. I wouldn't have had another child if W. hadn't been so keen. It wasn't a decision I'd have taken for myself alone. But my identity as a mother was still a comfortable one. I thought of myself as quite good at it. And I was glad she was a girl.

Now I have a grandchild. That strikes me as a joke really, my new identity as a grandmother, though I'm somehow proud too. I was weepy when the news came through. I suppose because it meant my son – though he hadn't lived with me for years – was now properly detached, part of a new family. He's been in America several years, and Sam was born there. It's rather sad seeing him only every six months. I can't watch him growing up, and the relationship is more tenuous than if they were in England. But being a grandmother – and older – will probably be freer than being a mother, when I think about it: there's more recognition and more room for your own needs and concerns, and you have more confidence in your right to be selfish sometimes.

Maybe my mothering tendencies explain why I'd be called

in to chair difficult sessions at conferences, for instance at the national women's liberation conferences. I'm quite good at exercising authority in a way that is seen as fair. I'm a placating person – try to forestall and avoid conflict, because it upsets me. I remember at Warwick a row with a man in a lift who was being snide about the Vietnam war. I remember being utterly infuriated, just within the course of going maybe three floors, by his indifference, and saying something violently angry, and coming out shaking. If pushed, I get enraged, but it's important to me to keep calm, though not to be silenced. I want to use the anger coherently and forcefully. Warwick was exciting because I found I could speak out effectively in public, in seminars and meetings, then at the sit-ins and the big meetings of 1969. I wasn't afraid to take sides, but I thought, and still do, that positions are best advanced by going for something that everyone can handle, or most people can handle, rather than pushing polarizations.

I went to several women's liberation conferences after Ruskin, until one at Birmingham where I felt alienated. One reason was that when I gave my 'Imperialism and Motherhood' paper there was a woman who dismissed it as irrelevant and tried to insist we talk about ecology and the countryside instead. I may also have come across some vigorous separatists there, and would have found that threatening as well as politically worrying. It was a period of challenge to the socialist feminism I'd taken for granted. When we started our Warwick women's group, we'd had to fight off opposition from some socialist comrades, so I was quite firm that women needed autonomous organisation. I also felt some tensions, not about being a socialist, but about socialist organisations and sectarianism. At Warwick I only joined the Socialist Society, an umbrella organisation. I disliked the sectarian competition I saw, and was particularly turned off by the way that members of one sect (International Socialists) functioned as a cabal. I felt strongly that people of different groups had to be able to work together, and that they undermined that possibility. I was horrified by a visiting speaker, who after a good talk, treated well-intentioned, if naive, questioners as though they were hostile, and put them down rather than answering them. That was a left style which I didn't like. For me, feminism was partly about developing new styles of political discussion and activity (which – simplistically – I'd also have identified more with Maoism), in which you had to convince people, you couldn't hector them and put them down, you had to convert them almost. I didn't like the development of sectarian differences within the women's movement.

So the socialist feminist meetings of the mid-seventies were important to me: they were a collective process in which people were working out ideas, not competing to dominate with their particular version. At least that's how I was experiencing them. I wasn't involved in organizing them, and didn't feel I knew many of those who were. My memory is that I felt a bit on the outside, at least to begin with. But I definitely wanted there to be some sort of focus and forum for socialist feminists, and some of my friendships date from then. I don't think I thought about vanguards. I've never liked it as a term, ever. I've always associated it with people being arrogant. When I was at Warwick I was impressed by speakers from Solidarity, and some of their syndicalist and grass-roots organisational principles, though at their conference I was put off by the male leadership style. I was sympathetic to anarchism, especially from the late-nineteenth century reading I did at Warwick. At absolutely the same time I was reading the *Morning Star*, the communist daily, and friendly towards communists – maybe it seemed possible because there was so much more overlap and moving around in my historical reading. Certainly in feminism I liked the attempts to be anti-authoritarian and work at the local level. For the last twelve years I have lived in a self-managed (but not owned) housing co-operative, which is an expression of that preference.

Although the Oxford conference had been exciting, I never saw conferences as the most central feminist activity. After 1975 I didn't go to them. I would probably have said I didn't have much to contribute and didn't feel I gained much from them. But there were other reasons. I was doing too much else – pushing on with my thesis, teaching part-time, working on *History Workshop Journal*, and managing a tight budget and a household with a small child, though my older ones were a great help. My main feminist involvement was with the Feminist History Group (which I'd been in since we started it in 1972 – the support group I'd wanted); and I took part in various History Workshop activities, or the occasional demonstration. Other feminists were working locally or developing resources on particular issues, or setting up women's centres and women's studies courses. I knew such work was important, but historical research, and now teaching, were time-consuming. But another reason for avoiding the big conferences and discussions, I now think, was that new alignments were emerging, with angry new demands which seemed to be breaking up the sense of unity – however unrealistic – we'd previously drawn strength from. And I was scared by the increasing emphasis on sexuality, and especially on lesbianism.

I have no idea whether there were any lesbians at the Oxford conference, or whether lesbian issues were discussed. I expect they weren't, but I think my unawareness is historically significant, and from today's perspective, odd. I don't know. I'd probably have seen lesbianism as politically risky – we had to keep the image of feminism clean, so to speak! – and personally threatening, one of the issues I found 'difficult', like the late 1960s US pamphlet called 'The Myth of Vaginal Orgasm' which I'd managed to avoid discussing. Lesbianism came up in the Stratford women's liberation group I went to, when a woman (who I would now instantly

67

know as lesbian, but at the time I didn't) said she was fed up with the way the discussions left no space for her because we were all heterosexual and only discussed our experiences. Actually, I don't think we discussed sex much anyway, but we often talked about men, and children and housewife problems, as well as general issues of equal pay and legal rights. I remember being very surprised, and rather shocked, and a bit indignant – we all got on so well, and of course no one was prejudiced! I'm sure she was right, and I did have difficulty recognizing she was right. If she was the only lesbian in the group, and she probably was then, it would have been uncomfortable for her to talk about things specific to that experience and identity, and all we could have done was nod, or whatever – or so we'd have thought. We might not immediately have known enough to see similarities and common ground.

One bitter February night in 1971 another woman and I had been putting up posters for the International Women's Day demonstration; she stayed over, and we ended up making love. Well, it was a cold night, we'd been in scary deserted subways around Aldgate, high tension – would we get caught? Sexual excitement and curiosity brought us together. We were both at that point completely heterosexual. We were embarrassed the next morning, and haven't seen each other since. I've no idea where she is. I think there was generally a block for me in thinking sexually of my feminist (or other female) friends: they were sisters. My actual sisters and I were very close, and it seemed natural to look for more. Nevertheless, I spent another night with a woman several years later, this time a friend I knew to be lesbian, without the anxieties and tensions of the first time. Then in 1984, on a visit to Australia, I fell in love with J., a woman.

It was complicated when I first came back, because although I knew this was an incredibly important relationship for me, I couldn't decide whether I was now 'a lesbian'. I joined the Lesbian and Gay Centre; and I tried going to the

Lesbian History Group, but I didn't fit. I went to some meetings of a group called Sexual Fringe, which was opposing a faction at the Lesbian and Gay Centre which wanted to exclude some people because of dress. It wasn't that I wanted to wear black leather, jackboots or chains myself, but I didn't like the arguments used or the principle of exclusion. Representations are complicated, and insignia can be worn for subversion just as well as for support. The militant openness of Sexual Fringe was helpful; they weren't interested in labels and categories and provided a sort of base for me in a time of confusion. The problem was that the relationship with J. involved feelings, desires, and dynamics which were familiar from my other relationships. Did that mean I wasn't a real lesbian? I didn't feel that loving her would mean I never again felt attracted to a man. But should I anyway say to everybody, 'I'm a lesbian', even if I wasn't sure, because it might be cowardice if I didn't. After a while I just stopped bothering. Most people knew about me and J., and I wasn't escaping the problems which resulted. Anyway, I felt a dislike of labels in general, and especially of the one which seemed the best fit – bisexual. Why should I take on a new identity when I was still me?

Involvement in the feminism of the early 1970s was exhilarating and empowering. We learnt that our discontents and thirsts were not individual. We made friends. We shared a vision of how things could change, in our immediate circumstances and relationships, and in the whole society beyond. We took action, singly and together. It was a productive, creative period, with proliferating groups, classes, libraries and archives, centres and publications, and many of the ideas we worked out then have since entered 'common sense'. The analyses we developed certainly shaped my research, and my work has been enriched by feminist practices of sharing and of listening. My personal life might have been smoother if I had not been emboldened by feminism, but it would

69

probably not have been happier. My career, too, could have been more orthodox, but I don't regret its eccentricities.

Still, I can see now that though our sisterhood gave us strength, it was also what limited us. Our networking expanded our numbers and our influence, but it didn't extend our base. We were criticised for being all white and middle class: neither description was wholly true, but there was a real truth behind the criticism. As sisters we were too similar; or in stressing sisterhood and our common oppression and strengths as women, we repressed and ignored differences which should have been recognised. We knew about class difference, though we thought it could be overcome through working together, but we hardly noticed differences of ethnicity or sexuality, and to the extent we did, thought it was enough to be 'not prejudiced', thereby assuming the different were always other, and 'we' were all the same. The political – and personal – struggle now needs a larger, more diverse 'we', who will combine in resistance to all the overlapping oppressions. I hope I'll go on being part of that.

Janet Hadley

I was twenty at the Ruskin conference. I was living in West London, working in a bank. I left school in 1967, and in 1967 and 1968 I was at a college in Holborn which is now part of Central London Poly, doing a crash 'A' level course in Russian, because I was going to go to University the following year and do Russian and Spanish.

I had dissenting middle-class parents who both voted Labour. My mother is Jewish. Her parents were German. They came from Germany in the first ten years of the century, and she was born in 1910. My father wasn't Jewish. My parents split up when I was five. I stayed with my mother, except that I was sent away to school quite early. My mother was a sincere, but quirky, liberal Jew, who tried to keep some of the festivals. I used to come home from school on a Friday night and she would light the candles, and then she'd put roast pork and apple sauce on the table. She did try. She tried to make me do the synagogue's correspondence course for children to learn Jewish history. When I was about twelve or thirteen I said I didn't want to do any of this, because I didn't believe any of it. I didn't have a strong awareness of myself as having a Jewish identity. I had considered myself anti-Tory since I was about fourteen, since the 1964 election, which was my political waking up, really. I remember being

71

incredibly excited when Harold Wilson won the election in 1964, and thinking, 'This is going to be really good now and things will be much "fairer".' A sort of fourteen-year-old appreciation of politics. So I was predisposed, if you like, to being enthusiastic about student revolution.

In 1968 I got involved with a man, much older than me, who'd been a Marxist for years and years. 1968 was quite an interesting year to be at college in Holborn. We were on the doorstep of the London School of Economics, one of the centres of student activism, and I just kind of got swept along into it, and was there at the LSE in the summer of 1968 and the student occupations.

The interesting thing about the man I got involved with what that he was Black; West Indian, first generation; he'd come here in 1956. It's important politically, because it was the time of Black Power, and I went to a lot of meetings with him and heard Stokeley Carmichael and listened to people talking about Black Power. Anyway, he was much older than me, and he was incredibly excited about what was happening politically, because he felt he'd been waiting for so long for this to happen. So I was involved from the sidelines in Black politics and Black Power, and especially the stuff about internalised oppression, and the whole question of identity, and colonialism and so on.

At first, before the notion of women's oppression dawned on my brain, I suppose I just felt very guilty and culpable, because I was white, and I was also from a privileged background, undoubtedly. I had had a private education, one of the pukka but liberal girls' boarding schools.

It was definitely an awakening – it was also an incredibly exciting time. The Black Panthers (a Black Power group that began in America) were starting up here, and people were coming from the West Indies describing the political goings-on there. I lived in Notting Hill. I also remember in May 1968 going to the home of C. L. R. James, the very distinguished West Indian Marxist historian and political activist, and

72

hearing him talk about the events in Paris. He was drawing parallels between the flight of de Gaulle, the president of France, when he left Paris and went to his country home, and the flight of the French king Louis the however-many-it-was, XVI I think – who left Paris in a closed carriage during the French Revolution and was stopped at the border of France. A lot of that evening went completely over my head, but I was *there*, listening to C. L. R. James, with his incredible wide-sweeping perspective on European history. You know, when you come back to re-read novels that you first read as an adolescent, you see all sorts of things in them that you had completely been unable to understand. Particularly sexual references, probably as a teenager you probably hadn't any notion they were there because they were subtle, addressed to adults. I had this strong feeling that I only understood a part of what was being said. Slightly bemused. Though I probably appeared very self-confident.

There were also these series of radical student conferences. I remember one in Manchester that I went to as well. They were fantastic, euphoric. There really was a feeling that we could change things. And also the excitement of the debate – there you were, you launched yourself off to Manchester in a bus, and you didn't know where you were going to sleep that night, but you were going to sit up and talk till two in the morning, and smoke too many cigarettes, and feel as if you were doing something. It was exciting.

When I first came across the notion of *women*'s oppression, I felt I already had a whole box of concepts that I could relate it to. I could say, 'oh yes, it's just like with Black people, women feel inferior, they're taught to feel inferior by society', and so on. I first heard about it at the University of Essex, where they had something in the winter of 1969 called the Festival of Revolution, talks, discussions, music and theatre. I went along on my own.

I was working as a bank clerk at that time. I had decided I wanted to do sociology. I had to earn my living for a year

73

while waiting to see if I could get into a university or polytechnic to do sociology. That's when I got a job in an old-fashioned bank, in Trafalgar Square. I used to sit in this bank – it's funny really – we had to wear green nylon overalls, and I worked in the income tax department, and my job was to fill in tax forms for incredibly rich people to help them pay as little income tax as possible. Then at the weekend I would go off to events such as the Festival of Revolution at Essex University. Not wearing green nylon overalls. Jeans, I expect.

I remember this moment at the Essex Festival – one of those moments in my life where I did something which I look back on and think, how on earth could I do that? Have the nerve to, I mean. It was in a steeply-banked lecture theatre, and we were all in these rows with desks, and I remember this woman giving a paper, which looking back on it, would be regarded as so commonplace now, about little-girl socialisation, the education system, the family and the division of labour in the home – and, I don't remember exactly what I said, but I remember standing up, interrupting this thing, which was a fairly kind of right-on thing to do, and saying, 'Sisters,' (this was a mixed audience of course, and nobody had ever heard of having women-only meetings), 'what we ought to be doing is discussing this amongst *ourselves*' – or something like that. Guffaws from the men. And there was this poor woman in the middle of giving her paper – and somebody said, 'Sshh, let the woman finish.' The next day, it was decided that women who wanted to would have a meeting on their own, without men, to discuss the oppression of women.

We had this meeting. Excluding men seemed very daring. I can't remember discussing much except whether or not men should be admitted. I think probably the reference back to Black separatism gave me courage to see that women *should* organise on their own. Blacks kept saying they should organise on their own, they ought to have Black power to do things on their own, they couldn't any longer organise in the way they had done during the civil rights movement. I was very easily able to make the leap to seeing that women were oppressed, and they couldn't ask men to liberate them. I wouldn't claim any originality or particular courage for it. It was just because I'd had this other experience, I suppose it was much easier for me to see. Then other parallels, such as gay liberation, came along afterwards.

As a result of that – I don't quite know how these things happened, I don't remember the mechanics of it or the decisions – a meeting was held about a month after the Festival of Revolution in a house in Shepherds Bush. It was a Sunday afternoon. It was in a small room, and it was one of those meetings where the door keeps opening and people keep moving up a little bit more and in the end they're all standing around the room and others are sitting with their knees up to their noses. I see that meeting as the start of the Women's Liberation Workshop. Somebody said there was a group of American women meeting in Tufnell Park, or Dartmouth Park. They were mostly anti-Vietnam war activists.

At some point the idea cropped up to put stickers on some very offensive swimwear advertisements on London Transport, and we had these stickers made. We used to get up at about five in the morning and go round London Transport tube stations, no doubt looking incredibly conspicuous, furtively getting our fingernails between the black plastic and the sticky paper, and we'd go up the moving escalator, and if you missed the swimwear poster you were up the top before you had chance to do it! I think the stickers prompted a little piece in *The Observer*, which then gave an address for Women's Liberation, which people could contact.

We did lots of things that summer. We started to produce the newsletter called *Shrew*. At first it was named something else; there was this kind of crazy idea that we were going to call each issue by different titles. We also did a hilarious thing, of going to Dickens & Jones department store at Oxford Circus and trying to zap the swimwear modelling. The idea was that we would conduct a funeral – it might have been something like Miss Nelbarden or something, we were going to bury. We assembled all the bits for the 'body' in the room that I was living in just off Notting Hill Gate. We got a big egg box, one of those giant ones from the supermarket, and that was going to be the coffin. Somehow we made this body out of balloons, and it had a red head and two huge red balloons. We'd got this very 'naughty' piece of black lingerie with cut-outs for the nipples on this balloon body. It was all very rickety. We got it onto the tube in the box, and at about Lancaster Gate one of the tits punctured, and it didn't look nearly so good after that.

We were going to do a 'street theatre' and we had to get into the Ladies of the restaurant on the fourth or fifth floor of Dickens & Jones; in the cubicles we had to change into black jumpers and black trousers or tights, and we were going to produce this thing, declaim this doggerel about Miss World, and the exploitation of women as 'sex objects'. 'Sex objects' was a phrase we used a lot. Sex objects was what the London Transport campaign was about. I don't really remember too much after that. Probably sheer terror blanked out my mind, after the business of trying to wrestle this thing in and out of the toilet door, changing clothes and getting to the swimwear department without being stopped by security. I think we attempted about thirty seconds' worth of this before we were pounced on and asked to leave. Two minutes later we were standing on the pavement in Regent Street feeling a bit 'deflated'. Weeks of planning and excitement had gone into it all. If there was any high-flown philosophy behind it, it certainly passed me by.

Going back to Black Power – I think it's quite important to say – as a personal memory I remember feeling fantastically relieved to find that *women* were oppressed and that I felt really passionately about this, because it gave me something

76

at home that didn't just leave me the out and out villain, an accomplice in the history of white supremacy. But I argued with my partner all the time. I went stridently into the home with women's liberation politics. Just because you're Black it doesn't mean that you don't have to do the dishes, and that it's OK for you to shrink my sweater to a size that would only fit a six-year-old, when you grudgingly attempt to do the washing at the launderette. And so on, and on.

I don't remember anything about the lead up to Ruskin. In 1969 I had been involved in the setting up of the Women's Liberation Workshop, and there was a group which met in Barnsbury Road, Islington, which in the course of that summer met up with a group of housewives in Peckham, and a group in Belsize Lane. During that autumn as far as I remember, those three groups got to know of each other's existence.

I have a vague recollection of somehow arriving in Oxford, but now it's as if by magic carpet. And this tremendous scrum of pre-conference organising, people trying to get themselves sorted out and find out the geography of the place. Where was the food, where were you going to put your sleeping bag that night. All that. It wasn't by any means my first 'revolutionary conference'. I felt an old hand by then, I suppose. One of the things that was new about it was that there were all these *children*, and there was going to be a creche, run by *men*. And I remember the fact that it was in two places. Part of it was at Ruskin and part in the Oxford Union. We knew it was going to be the first ever women's conference. My man didn't go.

I don't remember anything very much except the extra-ordinary powerful presence of this woman who was able to put into words things that made you say to yourself, 'That's what I've always thought and felt and I've never been able to put my finger on it.' At least one of the things that was talked about at that workshop was the whole relationship between women's oppression and Black oppression. There were Black women at the conference. My experience as a white woman in a Black Power context had been one of learning to be extremely respectful and careful towards Black women, because very often the whole question of Black men and white women was a fairly explosive issue. I didn't really have any close relationships with Black women at that time.

In the Oxford Union I remember there was a long table at the end of the room and these big windows behind, and the door halfway down, and people coming and going. It was the first time there had been a conference consisting mainly of women to discuss women's oppression or women's liberation, call it what you will.

After the conference I got much less involved, though I don't regard myself as ever having left the women's movement. But by this time I was a student again, on a sociology course, and I had some exams at the end of the first year, for which I hadn't done a stroke of work. Some choices faced me, so I sort of trailed off. I got my degree. Then I didn't know what to do so I foolishly went and did a post-graduate teaching course. It was a bit of a mistake. I had a spectacular, disastrous nine-week career as a teacher in a secondary modern school. Some time after half term I realised if I didn't get out a nervous breakdown was waiting for me. So I left.

I went and worked for 'Gingerbread', the self-help group for single parent families. Then I worked for SACU, the Society for Anglo-Chinese Understanding.

After SACU I went into journalism. I hadn't ever thought that being a writer was what I wanted to do. I began working on a health paper and I realised that this was really good fun. I've always been interested in making things happen. One of the attractions of going to work for the health paper, to do with consumers in the health service, was that it was about trying to change things and make things a bit more decent and bearable in this country. I really couldn't take any longer the removed politics of Maoism and also all the posturing of many of the Maoists who were associated with SACU at that time, telling workers in Sheffield to emulate Chairman Mao.

My personal relationship lasted for ten years. Without it I think I would have had a very different twenties. I would have travelled, for example. He hadn't got any money, and I hadn't enough for two of us. People always say, 'I always remember the day President Kennedy was shot.' My life is marked by memories of what Enoch Powell's 1968 speech against Black immigration meant. It meant that going on public transport and being around London became an experience of sheer terror for us, for weeks following that. Also when he was alone I was terrified for him, for his safety.

Women Against Racism and Fascism was formed in 1976. It was the time that the Anti-Nazi league was beginning to get active. It was the first thing for years that I'd actually felt moved to go along and really get personally involved in. Of course I'd been on the abortion marches. I had been on the first big women's liberation demonstration in 1971, on International Women's Day, the one with that wonderful poster. On the march were a group of women with a record player. It played 'Keep Young and Beautiful, if You Want to be Loved'. So I was there on demonstrations, the marches, the anti-immigration things, all those sorts of things. I never felt I was out of touch, but I didn't get involved in a group. But at last, in 1976, I thought right, Women Against Racism and Fascism, this is really something I *can* put my energy into, it says something to me. Obviously it brought together things that I felt very strongly about.

Out of that group came some events called Socialist-Feminist Educationals. It was still at a time when there were national women's conferences. With the usual hiccups. Anyway, some time in the winter of 1978, Women Against Racism and Fascism decided to come together with Women in Ireland (or was it Women and Ireland?), and produce one of these 'Educationals', on Imperialism, Immigration and

79

Racism. I got very involved in that. Organising it, writing papers. We split up into three groups, and in each group there were representatives of both Women in Ireland and Women Against Racism and Fascism. I was in a group trying to decide what racism was and where Ireland fitted in to racism. We wrote several papers. I wrote a paper on Depo-Provera, a drug that was being used as an injectable contra-ceptive on Black women, significantly in *this* country, which is one of the reasons it seemed relevant. It offered some hope for making some kind of meaningful alliances with Black women and supporting them.

Sally Alexander

I was a student at Ruskin College, Oxford, in spring 1969. I was doing the new history course, but I'd started off studying for a diploma in politics and economics. Ruskin's a college for trade unionists, and on the diploma course there were only two women that year, myself and Arielle Aberson, a Swiss woman, who died in a car accident in the summer of 1970. We were at the History Workshop, a huge conference of historians: students, academics, working people, informal, a very friendly atmosphere – in the coffee breaks and tea breaks people clustered and there was a suggestion that a group of women should get together and talk about the papers at the conference and whether or not there should be a women's history conference.

Sheila (Rowbotham) made an announcement at the end of a big plenary – it was such a striking moment for me. We were in the hall at Ruskin, both the hall and the platform were packed, a bunch of us – 'us' meaning women – on and around a table on the platform and Sheila made this announcement, and she said, 'We thought it would be a good idea if anyone here who was working on women's history . . .' – and there was a roar of laughter. There were just shrieks of laughter. At first, instead of being angry, I felt embarrassed.

Then I can remember filing out of the room. The men were apologetic, not laughing quite so much after Anna (Davin) had told them off. I think we all murmured to each other, 'What was so funny about that? Did we say something wrong?' But people did come up, they were interested. I remember a couple of American women, who seemed incredibly self-confident and articulate, compared to us. We all agreed that there *should* be a conference on women's history. The one thing I remember about that first meeting is the atmosphere, lots and lots of people all dressed in sweaters and jackets and tweed coats – it was very crowded everywhere, and the room was crowded with women. Ruskin bedrooms were small, so there didn't have to be very many people in there, maybe fifteen or twenty, for it to be absolutely packed, and there was a lot of excitement, and a lot of smoking, and coming and going. People from all different parts of the country saying, 'We can have a paper on this' and 'We can do that', 'We can organise this', 'We can have a three-day conference, completely on the history of women, and we can find out lots of information.' And that was how it was conceived. I was in a central position because I was a Ruskin student, but I didn't know very much history, or how to organise a conference.

I was married in 1964. I had my daughter Abigail in 1965. I went to the Royal Academy of Dramatic Art when I was sixteen – that was in, what, 1959. Then I went into the theatre and did jobs in rep. Then I married and after marriage I didn't really work very much. I was a woman of the early sixties. Or a girl – we were girls then, weren't we? My husband was an actor, and all my friends were people like writers and directors and their girlfriends and wives, and people who were on the left, men who were on the left. They were all much more political, much more articulate than I, they were all university educated, and neither my husband nor I were.

In London I got involved in helping to set up *Black Dwarf*, which makes me sound far more politically sophisticated than I was. A friend, Clive Goodwin, had asked me to help. The women – the 'girls' in the office of *Black Dwarf* – we ran around. I would be told to go and raise money – 'Go to this theatre producer, Sally, and don't leave his office till he's signed a cheque for £10' – that sort of thing. All the women were like me, raising money, doing the secretarial work, doing the helping, sitting around, having affairs with the men or not. Perhaps there was the occasional woman writer, or perhaps a very wealthy woman, society woman or something.

There was one striking exception. One day, when I was licking and addressing envelopes, sitting on the floor in someone's bedroom, Sheila Rowbotham came in. She was quite different. She had been to Oxford, for one thing, she had a sense of politics, history – she knew more politics than most of the men. She wrote. She was an extraordinary woman. I'd never met anyone like her in my life before. But I was not like that. It was 1968, I was twenty-five, Abigail was three, I'd been married and divorced. I was having a very intense and painful affair, and I felt very, very silent. I once asked L. – this man with whom I was having an affair, 'What do you really want to do?' and he said, 'I'd like to be a pop singer, and I'd like to lead a revolution from the hills' – and that was his serious reply. I think I made some stupid remark. I didn't have the words or the language to argue against him.

My father was a self-made man, and he was determined that none of his children should ever suffer, and when my marriage broke up, he said he would give me an allowance, which he did. I wanted to be a bohemian when I was a girl, an adolescent. It was the late fifties and my family had no intellectual aspirations. I wanted to wear black, and be a bohemian, I didn't really know what that meant. When I went to RADA it was all those films – Truffaut, Bergman, Fellini, Antonioni.

83

I never took to make-up because my older sister wore make-up a lot, and every time she came downstairs in her evening frock and purple eye shadow and thick mascara and red lipstick, my father would have a nervous breakdown and there'd be a major row. I was two years younger, and I thought there is no way I'm going through that rubbish with my father, I want to go to live in Paris; I was into open-necked white shirts and black sweaters and short cropped hair and no make-up. I didn't want to waste my arguments, I thought there should be no hanging, and I wanted homo-sexuals to be legalised – and I didn't want my father to be wasting his time arguing with me about whether I wore make-up. Also, I was a tomboy – I'd wanted to be Lord Byron when I was thirteen, then I'd wanted to be Davy Crockett when I was eleven, and I wanted to be Marlon Brando in 'On the Waterfront' when I was fifteen.

I'd obviously done quite a lot by the time I was at Ruskin, at that meeting. Clearly there was some gap between my self-presentation and how I actually felt inside. What I felt inside was inarticulate, but enthusiastic, if timid. But on the other hand, I had some experience of politics, I knew the names of the different groups! Sheila, for one thing, at this memorable session sitting on the floor sticking envelopes, had given me a map of the left wing groups. Nobody else would have given me the time of day. Those men I knew then – I'd say 'But I haven't read Marx,' and I remember one of them saying to me 'How old are you, Sally? Can you read?' When I asked Sheila something like that she answered my questions. She'd tell me all about everything. I thought that was wonderful. There was also a certain amount of guerilla warfare between the women and the men at that time. You were having affairs with the men, and they were both passionate and antagonistic, so you were involved in that sort of sexual antagonism. But the real friendships were with people of your own sex.

When I went to Ruskin I was thrown into a different

environment, it was all male trade unionists – and again I was completely silent in every meeting and every seminar. I'd moved from knowing working-class men with chips on their shoulders, to writers on the left in the theatre, to trade unionists and members of the Labour Party and the Communist Party, who had a very powerful political culture and way of speaking to each other, from which I was completely excluded, but this didn't strike me as odd at all.

I was impatient for something – life, I suppose. I had liked the London people, they were doing things. They were going to theatres all the time, going to movies, talking about ideas. Some had been at Oxford or other universities together, or in National Service. The men (without money!) came from working-class backgrounds. I really liked them. I wanted to do something with my life, I didn't know what, and how I got to be a student at Ruskin was an accident. Someone suggested it to me. I didn't know what I was going to do. I went to the interview, wrote an essay and I got in. When I got there, it was a devastating shock. It was a very traumatic decision, a decision almost out of desperation. I had to leave the world I was in, I didn't like being a 'bird', it wasn't right. It wasn't that I didn't like those people. I still like them . . . .

I think now that there was no way to be a woman and to be intelligent and articulate in the sixties. If you wanted to identify with a rebel when you were growing up in the late fifties and early sixties, the rebels were young men like Albert Finney. So the vocabulary was masculine. The women's and men's worlds were quite separate in a way. There weren't many women I knew then who were politically knowledgeable. One of the reasons I wanted to go to Ruskin was that I was interested to know more about the Labour Party and the trade-union movement. Within two years I knew the history of the labour movement, all the names of the trade unions, the character of them, the inner struggles. My own first lessons in class politics had been meeting my husband and going into the theatre. In my first job in rep I was made to

85

feel, in no uncertain terms, that I was privileged. But I'd learned that at grammar school. I was treated there as if I was very rich. Not posh, but rich. I was taken away and sent to a small boarding-school, because I was ill, I had polio when I was thirteen. I left at fifteen because there was nothing else to do. I got my 'O' levels. So, I qualified for Ruskin because I'd left school at fifteen. And I'd been in a trade union, I was in Equity. When I went to RADA at sixteen – I got in out of the blue, nobody expected me to get into RADA, like I got into Ruskin later – I've since learned that I'm good at first impressions!

I had a powerful social conscience. I did voluntary work when I was a young woman in London, but it didn't cohere into a political theory or strategy at all, until the women's movement. There are two things I'd say about my own political innocence. One is that I'd read nothing, nothing. I'd read novels. I tried to read *The Feminist Mystique* (Betty Friedan) because a woman friend suggested it, but I couldn't finish it. She gave me *The Divided Self* (R. D. Laing) and I read one chapter of that. I just didn't have any way of reading something like that. I felt extremely ignorant. I am one of the women writers who's read by other people now, so I know the difference. There was a blank, the space where concepts and ways of putting things together is now! I'd read masses of nineteenth-century novels. There's this impression that I have of myself, this rather dreamy, timid, silent person. That's what it felt like. Sort of wafting around.

When I was at Ruskin, there were about a hundred men and two women, and the men were engineers and miners, from every sort of manual trade, and had a trade-union history. They'd left their wives and children at home. So we women had a very high profile. I didn't blossom in that direction. One or two of the men became close friends but a lot of them didn't know how to relate to me. Organising the women's history conference at Ruskin meant that I was very preoccupied with the students at Ruskin and how they would take it, how we – Arielle and I – would get it through the Students Union, all of which seemed like an absolute nightmare to me at the time. I didn't know what a student union was or how you managed to stand up and speak.

Fortunately Arielle, although younger than I was, was far more politically sophisticated. She was also very vital – a very alive person – much loved and respected at Ruskin. She'd come from a Communist family. I had this experience at Ruskin on my very first night there, when you're meant to stand up and say where you came from. I'd said that I was a housewife and mother. The men laughed.

Both my parents came from Reading. My father came from the back streets of Reading, a very unrespectable family, his father was a greyhound bookie. He wanted his daughters to be respectable and middle class, and so we became. But our culture is the culture that he gave us, which is music-hall jokes and Frank Sinatra and Bing Crosby. It was clearly there in me, that sense of class difference. When I met my husband, at one level you could say it was the 'Look Back In Anger' marriage. The middle-class girl marrying the working-class boy.

I went to some of the meetings held to organise the Ruskin Conference. Originally it was going to be a Women's History Workshop, which would have been relatively straightforward, but then it was decided that it would be a women's liberation conference. My next memory is of going to a meeting somewhere in London. Unlike the Ruskin meetings, which were dark and full of smoke and people, this meeting was light, and there was sun, and a lot of women. I really liked it, it was a quite, quite different atmosphere. I remember women who just passed as kind of images in front of me, and a lot of giggling. I felt completely at home. I'd been to an all-girls school, all my life, always surrounded by women, dozens and dozens of women friends – my husband used to call my friends the female Mafia. I think I took that as a joke. To find myself in these meetings doing something, instead of being silent and rather bored and frustrated, or making the tea or listening to the men, and only talking to your women friends afterwards – this was wonderful. I didn't do any deciding or choosing. I knew nothing, and I was quite happy not to.

It actually took me years, years, to reach the point where I thought I could take responsibility. In fact, I can't even remember who did make all the decisions, but I do remember that Arielle and I were treated rather like the dogsbodies on that. I didn't mind, except when those young situationists painted slogans, and then I was furious. All over the college. I can't remember the slogans. Well, we had to clean it up. It was eight o'clock in the morning. One of the students phoned me and said, 'We cannot ask the cleaners to clean this mess.' I was furious: that they should expect women cleaners to clean this wretched mess up. I was absolutely enraged. I couldn't give a damn about the politics. All I remember was the police coming and going, and everybody wanting to have long conversations with me about the politics of the women who'd done it. I couldn't have cared less what their politics were. I didn't want them to get into trouble with the police, I did know that. There was a lot of whispering in corners, and dramas, oh God. It's like with children – who do you think's going to clean that bloody mess up? Me.

Arielle and I cleaned the whole college. The blokes helped us. The male students. Sunday morning. Afterwards there was about six months' struggle with the authorities and the male students, who were furious at what had happened. The students were enraged at their college being taken over by all these women, all these children, at the mess, at the disruption, at the slogans being painted – most of them weren't anti-male at all, but this particular group of women were very hostile to men, very aggressive. 'Our college has been messed up, it was taken over by this bunch of women, too disruptive; we couldn't watch sport' – this was the main thing. They couldn't go into the television room and watch sport. Women were streaming all over the college, causing disruption. It should never be allowed again. I was frightened. It was funny when you sat and talked about it, but then when you went into a meeting it was like a lot of politics, you know how it is, you think these issues are quite funny, but people actually hold their positions with tremendous strength of feeling and rage.

The complaints about the television room and the mess were a cover for something which seemed really very disruptive and threatening. Some of the students were opposed to the History Workshops anyway, because they were democratic jamborees. We had to defend them, so that they could continue to be held at Ruskin. I think that was the first time I'd ever made a political speech. I couldn't possibly tell you what I said. I was carefully briefed by Mac Reid, a Ruskin student, who handled the Union, presented the defence of the women's conference, but eventually compelled Arielle and myself to speak on our own behalf. I could never write anything in those days, not even notes for a talk. I just spoke. I practised what I was going to say. It was something very short, like, 'It was the first ever National Women's Conference and it was very important, the politics were democratic. I know it was very disruptive but it was only for two days . . .' I tried to make the links between the kind of college Ruskin was and women's oppression.

The conference was very exhilarating. There was a tremendous sense of achievement that Arielle and I both felt. After the first session got going, Arielle and I went to the pub and had a drink. It was all, 'Isn't this amazing? We've done it!' We didn't want to go to hear any papers at first, we were too tired. We couldn't believe it. Everyone was very friendly and warm, and we made friends with lots of people.

I remember there was this long discussion on the Friday evening about whether men should be allowed in or not. I felt that they shouldn't. I felt I didn't want them there, I just didn't know why. I didn't know what the political justification for it was.

Mostly my memories are of organising the conference, worrying about all that side of things, endless wasted time with the police about these wretched women who'd painted these slogans. Also dashing backwards and forwards picking Abigail up. I must have felt there was a sense of purpose and mission in doing something important. Because I wasn't properly an intellectual at all, and didn't know how to absorb information, the actual content of the conference mostly passed me by. As an event, it was mind blowing. We'd done it. That was a shared feeling. It felt like the culmination of something. It didn't feel like the absolute beginning. I think from that moment bits of myself became more together. I think I became more myself. I think I came out more. And I never went back to – or was ever remotely interested in – those sorts of bits and pieces of male left politics that I had picked up on and had seen a bit of.

I was a socialist, but it seemed that the women's movement was the place to be a socialist, and my socialism and the women's movement just came together for me in a way which now, I must admit, is no longer clear. In that now, I can see how it is possible to be both a socialist and a feminist, but there's no necessary connection between the two. It's possible now for very conservative women to be feminists. That didn't seem possible at all then. The WLM was democratic and revolutionary. I think there was a discussion at that first Friday evening meeting, where someone said, 'But isn't an all-women's meeting reformist?' And I thought, what's she talking about? I didn't know what that distinction was, between reform and revolution – I thought then that the connections for me were very clear. I think that was something to do with the emphasis in the women's movement on organising from where you are.

One of the legacies of the sixties, or perhaps it was one of the legacies of the women's movement, is that you don't organise other people, you don't go out there and organise the working class, which always seemed patronising and very arrogant of young male lefties that I met at Oxford. The ones at the university were younger than I was and they were right-on Marxist socialists, in the left-wing groups and talked about class all the time. That never worked for me as a political vocabulary. Because I was a woman, I knew how to work with them, but I was never one of them. I didn't want to go out there and organise all these working-class people. I wanted to do it from where I was, which is of course what feminism has always emphasised historically.

Ruskin changed my whole life. It helped me find myself. I felt very comfortable with the identity of the women's movement. My intellectual work at Ruskin was also very interesting for me and I got better at it. All my life I was a classic feminist. That generation, you know, where fathers came home from the war and we never got over it. All through my childhood I was told that I was too clever by half, and it was never going to do me any good. I would never get married. 'You're far too attractive, Sally, to let on to men how clever you are' – that's what my father said and he still says it.

Men did things. Unlike women. They went out, and they took taxis across London, they travelled, they wrote plays. They thought, 'Let's go on holiday', and they got into cars and drove off. I wanted to do things. I really did. I also wanted to have children, and be married. Very much. I still think that's the real problem for women, it's terribly hard to do both.

I learned who I was through the women's liberation movement. A child of the welfare state, I was born into the right to education, subsistence, housing and health – that birthright gave my generation the confidence to expect more. I was also a rebel, a tomboy, the infant who had never recovered perhaps from my father's returning from the war and taking my place in my mother's bed.

We didn't want to be wives, to stay at home, to do the

housework (feminists have hated housework since at least the seventeenth century). We wanted – we said – economic independence, a body liberated from the projections of men's lusts, a 'language of our own'. The more prosaic demands for nurseries, equal pay, abortion and contraception on demand seem even more vital today for millions of women and children.

I learned that women are different from each other, with differences that can be corrosive of respect, love, mutuality; that feminists can be greedy in their wish for everything – jobs, money, love, children, husbands, loves. I learned that none of us live outside ideology. I was enthralled at that idea. It seemed a revelation! To explain both the limits of one's own thoughts – how difficult to circumvent cliche – but also the materiality of speech and thought. Ideas we believed were as powerful – certainly they were as exhilarating – as economics. And I learned too that ideas can become harsh taskmasters, they can mutilate, moralise, divide people.

I still want people to want more, to devise forms of democracy which could implement the first and shared political demands of the WLM. Some habits of thought have been changed – my son returns from school speaking of 'the man or woman who drives the fire engine' – children educated in comprehensive schools do seem to me to have a social generosity that earlier generations lacked. I'm proud of the cultural achievements of feminism but look back on our political audacity with wonder.

How to legislate for real change in relations between the sexes, for the elimination of poverty, or more and more democracy, seems now less clear. I hope my fears, and Margaret Thatcher's determination to be rid of socialism in thought and deed, haven't made me, or too many of my generation, politically quiescent.

Janet Ree

We'd moved into a new house about two weeks before Ruskin. I was seven months pregnant, unmarried, and very at sea. I'd been living in a flat in Victoria with friends and the lease had come to an end and we'd had to move. I'd had to go round looking for somewhere to live, very pregnant, and not wearing a wedding ring – I seemed to feel it was important not to wear a ring, not to pretend I was something I wasn't – and got a lot of very frosty responses, especially from women.

I had always assumed through my childhood and adolescence and young womanhood that I would be a wife and mother with several children. But when I did get pregnant it was unintentional and I was in a not very satisfactory relationship with a man I didn't know very well. He then announced that he didn't believe in marriage on principle and that he would never marry, and he didn't approve of the state interfering with relationships. Having a baby made no difference. If I wanted him to stay with me he always would, but if I didn't want him to, then he wouldn't. I'd never come across such an argument, it seemed quite incredible to me at the time.

I stopped writing diaries when I got pregnant. Until the time when I found I was pregnant and decided I would have the baby, the diaries are full of anguished feelings about not being able to talk to him, feeling his politics were completely unconnected with anything to do with me. He was involved in *Black Dwarf* and what was happening in 1969, but wasn't part of the libertarian left at all. He was quite a loner. We went together to socialist meetings, and after one I wrote that I cheered along with the rest but I felt inside I was absolutely detached from what was going on. I wrote in capitals in the diary – 'Where was I. Where was me?' I felt fantastically ashamed of feeling that, because I thought that was the last thing I should have been thinking about when world revolution was on the cards. The idea that my little world might not have been represented seemed very unacceptable. That's why it was put in the diary.

When I got pregnant and stayed unmarried, my grandfather, who I really adored and was very close to, cut me off and refused to see me again. It was awful. I saw him once more, just before he died, a year later. My own father, who has liberal views on the whole, even he was disturbed. This was 1969. I didn't know anyone who'd had a baby and not got married; I hardly knew anyone who'd had a child at all, actually.

I'd finished at Oxford in 1965. Then I got cancer and had to have a year at home, then I did a year at the London Institute of Education, then a year school-teaching. In 1968 I did a diploma in social and cultural studies at Chelsea Tech. And for six months after that I worked for Thames Television. During that time, in late 1969, I got pregnant. I'd had quite extensive radiation treatment after my operation four years earlier, so I was warned by the doctor that there was a possibility I wouldn't have a normal baby and I was offered an abortion. He said – my partner, he was very correct in all these ways – he said, 'It's your decision. I'm not going to put any pressure on you.' I knew, actually, he would have preferred me to have the abortion. I knew he thought we weren't really suited. I suppose I felt terribly confused. I felt very friendless. I'd always had very close women friends but I didn't have any then, or at least not in London. My mother had died when I was eighteen. I was very close to her, and I think I've still never really come to terms with her death. I missed her fantastically at this time. My two brothers were not around. I wished, as I often did and do, that I'd had a sister. My world seemed dominated by men.

Anyway, that was the context. I think I must have felt a bit like some of today's teenagers do, the feeling that having a baby might give my life a purpose and that I'd be a good mother, and I would try to make something real and permanent. I'd always thought I'd marry a poet, and here I was with this most unpoetic man, a difficult person in many ways. But I knew he was a very principled man – I knew if he said he would never leave me, he wouldn't. So I decided to go ahead and have the baby.

We moved here, to this house in North London, in February 1970, just before Ruskin. It was a bleak and frightening time. I was very unhappy. During that time I remember very clearly I went to the British Museum one day and I met Sheila Rowbotham who I'd known at Oxford. Sheila was saying something like, 'You should take your own wishes seriously. I understand why you want to be married. Women have a right.' I'd told her how hard I was finding it, the hostility from the family – and in those days at the hospital, if you weren't married, they called you 'Miss'. I hated that conspicuousness and the disapproval. I remember her formulating the idea that women had a right to things like getting married if it made them feel better. I remember walking home in a kind of daze, as if someone had really hit me with some new perception. And Sheila told me about a women's conference at Ruskin. I had no idea what she meant. I didn't realise there'd been women's groups in London two years before that.

I'd been a member of various left groups since school – Young Socialists, the Labour Club at university, CND – but

95

this was the first conference I'd been to. The only thing I remember most clearly is sitting up in the gallery, totally on my own. I knew not a single person, and I felt myself to be a hundred per cent conspicuous, because I was very pregnant. The main body of the hall was full of people, and I watched them coming in and greeting each other, and I saw this woman, she was incredibly beautiful with this long white fur coat on, and there were people gathering around her. They seemed to be queuing up to talk to her. People were friendly to me eventually. There was a sense, which continued to be so important through every conference I then went to, of an openness and friendliness and a real attempt to smile at people who looked nervous. That kind of thing was really striking.

Most important of all to me was a re-jigging in my head of the importance of women. I remember women talking about housework, and child-rearing. I'd never really thought of housework. I knew my mother had been a housewife, but I didn't really have any particular resistance to it. It was really interesting hearing women saying they were fed up with it.

My partner's line on pregnancy was, women in China go on working till the minute they drop their babies, then go back to work. It was a sign of Western corruption to think of pregnancy as something you should be soft on. So I accepted that, and assumed there was nothing special about it either. It wasn't that the conference actually altered that, it just made different things important, and it was the first time I'd heard women talk about the things that affected their ordinary everyday lives. Some of them didn't have posh voices, they didn't have the usual rhetoric of the left – they could just have been anybody. Well, they were just anybody. I don't know who they were. There was a woman with a very upper-class accent who got booed from the stage. I felt quite sorry for her. But she was a bit silly, she got up and said she didn't believe in work and she had decided that work was oppressive to women, and people were yelling, 'Oh, I suppose Daddy's keeping you.' I saw how discomforted she was. She obviously felt she was making a valid point. If you were a woman, whatever you said, even if it was unacceptable like that, it was part of the sea of contributions.

Harriet was born at the beginning of May 1970. I had a very frightening, lonely time. I was in Westminster Hospital for two weeks, after a Caesarean, and during that time I had no visitors at all. I went back in September to teaching part-time at the Further Education college where I'd done my teaching practice. I put Harriet with a baby minder, came back and breast-fed her. I remember getting classes that were sufficiently dotted around to be able to come back.

Now, when I see and experience my women friends having children, it really strikes me how crucial that early Ruskin conference, and the subsequent formation of the group that met in my house, was for my perception of being a mother. The difference between the way I brought up Harriet, the way I brought up Becky four years later, the way women now focus upon their children – is very striking, and often distressing to me.

This may be unfair to what the women's movement was saying – I know people have said it's wrong to perceive the early women's movement as being against children and mothering, and I'm not saying it was actively against them. But what I did pick up as being really primary for women was to be yourself in your own right. And for mothers that meant not falling for the so-called myth of motherhood. I completely accepted this line. The demands we formulated, like the one for 24-hour nurseries, sprang from those beliefs that mothering oppressed women – and children too, in fact. The assumption was, it wasn't good for children to be too closely identified with the mother, that it was good for children to have working mothers whose lives weren't focussed only on them. But there was a clash for me, even though at the time I didn't allow it to surface. I loved family life – I wanted to re-create it along the lines of how my own

97

family had been before my mother died. It was a very conventional aspiration. And really the time was not right for those feelings of the family, not in the women's movement of the early seventies – or at least not in the socialist feminist part of it I identified with.

In a curious way, what I took as the feminist line on children and childcare was quite similar to my partner's. It was a bit how he felt about pregnancy – he reckoned children needed to be independent from early on, to know the world is a harsh place – that's what he used to say. Which isn't to say he wasn't a very devoted father – he was – but absolutely not indulgent. He didn't believe in toys, for instance. And crying – when they cried at night he'd be completely opposed to going to pick them up. They had to learn their desires wouldn't always be met. And that also seemed to tie in with the new feminist thinking about being in thrall to your children – you shouldn't sacrifice yourself to them. I think I was very confused about what was right. And they've turned out to be fantastic – my daughters – so maybe it wasn't such a bad thing. But I do feel sad about that time in many ways, I'd like to have enjoyed, and felt legitimate in, spending more time with Harriet when she was a baby. It's partly thinking I should have resisted, insisted more. But it was hard, the tide seemed to be going the other way.

Whatever else was lacking in my domestic set-up – and it certainly didn't get any easier to talk to my partner – he was great about things like sharing the housework, and really sharing it. We both worked half time. When I was out at one point four evenings a week at meetings, there was no problem, he would always babysit. I think all those aspects of feminism, the ones about work, responsibility for childcare, housework – all the things to do with changing structures, he really supported. In the groups I was in, very often the theme was the uncooperativeness of men, and women actually saying they'd had to escape through the back window to come to the meeting. I had none of that. I was very fortunate in that sense.

Going back to 1970, then, I went to a meeting in Hackney probably four or five months after Ruskin, when Harriet was a few months old. There were loads of women, about fifty, in a bedroom. Amazing. We were divided up. Those of us who had houses had to say if we had any room where we could meet. So I volunteered to have a group at my house. I remember coming away from that meeting with a sinking heart. Here were all these women whose names and addresses I'd taken, and the following Tuesday I'd agreed they would all meet here. I didn't know what on earth I'd taken on. I didn't know what a women's meeting was. I felt I needed instruction.

The important slogan for me was 'The personal is political'. Instead of feeling all the time that there was something called politics in which I'd been trying to insert myself, now there would be me, and something would be inserting itself – therefore, when I went to conferences, which always engaged me fully at a much more political level, the demands and the debates seemed to flow naturally from the percep- tions that I'd had that were completely subjective and to do with the changes in my life, as part of a couple, as a mother, and by then as a friend.

Talking to other women about fears and doubts and finding that they'd got the same ones, was absolutely fantas- tic. You had this feeling of being high, and somehow corpor- ate, part of something large, public and significant. It was wonderful. The best kind of relationship I've ever had. The feeling was like you have when you're in love. The world was re-made in the image of whatever you were in love with. A ridiculous hyperbole – but a sense which I find slightly hard to recapture, because it's now so normal. It was such a turbulent change.

But having said all that, the group which resulted from that Hackney meeting wasn't a great success. It went on for about two years. I used to get a lot of flak from some women who came, that I was just being a hostess. One woman stormed out because she said I was always trying to make people feel at ease and wished I would stop. I was always smiling at people. It was awful. She said she was fed up with people just sitting around, middle-class women not getting out and actually doing things. I felt she was completely right. I was a hostess – can you imagine, I always made cakes. And tea and coffee. I've always loved making a kind of home. All the peripheral things like cooking and sewing, having a nice warm room, all that. It was really important. But I was very mortified and recognised the justness of that description of myself. I might as well have been hosting the Women's Institute. That was the subtext.

There were twelve women, and at first I was the only one with a child. Then one other mother joined. But the last thing anybody talked about was what it felt like to have a baby or be a mother. That, I think, contributed to my perception that having a child was something that was not to get in the way of all these other more important things. There was a lot of talk about men, and a certain amount about women, having relationships with women, whether sexual or not, and talk of local campaigns and things.

I had Becky in 1974 – and by then the first group had folded and I was then a member of another group meeting round the corner, the Arsenal group. I was more at ease there. It was a more homogenous group – socially, I mean – for instance, everyone in the group had been to university, and most were, like me, in jobs like teaching. It was less confrontational than the first group had been. And the meetings were – well, they were absolutely fundamental, central to the week. It would have been unthinkable to miss one.

One meeting is specially memorable to me, and I think it was fairly crucial to the group itself. I'd had Becky in February 1974, and two days after I came out of hospital I went to a meeting. I was really excited that I was going to see everyone again. They were reading a paper that somebody had produced, on women in Eritrea. I arrived, late, at the meeting. Nobody looked up. I sat down, and I realised nobody was going to say anything to me about having Becky. I couldn't believe it, because these were good friends. After about three quarters of an hour, when nobody had said anything at all to me, I found myself crying, tears dropping onto the page, and I got up and went home. I was absolutely devastated. You know how funny you feel after you've had a baby. I'd had a Caesarean again, I was not well. Becky never stopped crying, night or day. I was longing to talk about it. To do them justice, several of them came round later in the week with flowers and things, and said that the next week I should take the meeting, and talk about the experience of having Becky. I remember I baked a cake – of course – and I talked. I know some of them remember that meeting still. Most of them have had children since. A fair amount of soul-searching went on, about the fact that they had totally ignored a woman who they felt warm towards – it wasn't that I took it personally, but there was no taking on what having a baby involved, physically, let alone emotionally. I think that began to change thereafter. We then made it a point, when people did begin to have babies, everybody was extremely supportive. We always went to see them in hospital.

I went to all the women's liberation conferences, from 1970 to 1975, I think. After that I went less often. I remember there was one after Becky was born, in 1974, which was somehow very troubled and unpleasant. Full of dissension. Probably then I did have a sense of there being two strands in the women's movement, that the women's liberation ones were more likely to be about sexual orientation – whether the women's movement was sufficiently attentive to lesbians. I'd found talking about gayness quite hard, but desirable at the same time. It was very circumscribed on the one hand, but on the other hand I knew, because in adolescence I had had sexual relationships with girls, that I had always found women extremely attractive. I found that whole area very disturbing and interesting, and yet at the same time quite alienating, when it was embodied with actual people and debates.

Then there were the socialist feminist conferences which were much easier. They were obviously more to do with demands and trying to formulate a future for women that the maximum number of women could agree to. I found those very stimulating. But I think I continued to feel the idea of being a mother was seen as second-rate and the whole notion of these twenty-four hour nurseries – and even abortion on demand, although there was no question but that I would support that politically, and still would – it was complicated. I'd always wanted lots of children, there was no question. I would hate to have had an only child. I remember a meeting where women were talking about the irresponsibility of bringing children into the world – maybe it was the ecology argument – overpopulation, or the nuclear threat, I don't know.

I felt it was something I had to justify, and that doesn't seem to come up at all now. I don't feel that women who now get pregnant have this agonised debate. The desire for a close relationship with a baby – I think now that is very clearly recognised. Whereas then, it was much harder to admit those feelings. Reading some of those early feminist manifestos, somehow the whole rhetoric is very raw, having come from mainstream left politics of the sixties, and then clashing head on with the personal, unworked-out regressive kind of feelings and desires for womanliness that many of us who were young in 1970 brought with us, presumably, from our fifties rearing.

Despite always feeling it didn't take on motherhood, I absolutely loved being in the women's movement. I've so many friends – friends is almost the wrong word. The quality of relationship that those meetings and groupings produced is indescribably powerful, and far more important than my relationship with a man was at that time, without question. Far more intense and loving, subtle, engaging, profound. I always found women easier than men, I still do. Towards the end of the seventies we had this mixed anti-sexist group. I'd always felt there was something about what happened to men when they shed their trappings of power – I somehow couldn't perceive them as attractive, so I brought this up at one of the meetings. Did sexual relationships between men and women depend on sexist feelings? It was difficult and murky, I could hardly bear to articulate it. Actually, what happened, most people got off with other people in the group!

I felt a bit mortified. Years later I talked to people about it, and I think there was something very peculiar going on at those meetings. The group had about six meetings, I think. It was such a relief to get back to the single sex groups, and have a laugh. It made you realise how you were still playing these games. I remember the other thing I said, which I always insisted on even in the women's groups, that I liked things about being feminine, I always liked wearing make-up, jewellery, nice clothes, I liked perfume, all these things, and I refused to give them up. It doesn't seem a big deal at all now, but then it was much more earnest. The truths were more simple, and therefore to dissent from them was a bit harder. There were certain things I felt defiant about.

I was never drawn to the part of the women's movement which denied the social and economic differences between women, and class. That's now gaining ground again, specially in the United States – or maybe it never went away – goddess worship, seeing the world in terms of myth, it's frightening, and undeniably powerful. Despite socialist feminists' shortcomings about mothering, I never felt I'd be more at home being revered as an earth-mother. Never. What was great about the women's movement as I saw it was that it never elevated self-preoccupation; even though it started from your own needs, it was constantly seeking connections with political and social realities, and possibilities.

The Ruskin conference, and then the women's movement, really made sense to me of how I wanted to live. Even though I continued to live in many ways quite conventionally (with two children, in a heterosexual couple relationship), inwardly it gave me a feeling of confidence, a feeling of power which I had never felt before in my life. Before 1970, I was completely bounded by men and male attitudes. After that, the whole thing reversed and it became my world, not my partner's. And ironically, my early misery at not being married, which he had insisted on and I had found so hard, came to be a wonderful cachet for me.

For instance, I remember going to some conference quite soon after Ruskin, in 1971 I think, and someone said, 'Is there anybody here in this hall who is actually an unmarried mother?' This was such an accolade, we wanted unmarried mothers to come to the movement, and they were rarer in those days. I put my hand up, and I was absolutely a star! I did actually admit that it wasn't really my decision, I couldn't really claim credit for it because I had so desperately wanted to get married. But within a year of this happening – obviously I'd never called myself Mrs anything or worn a ring – I felt that was the objective correlative, that was the proof that I was somebody who was a really proper feminist. I always thanked him for that. By the time I got pregnant with Becky, I had the perfect combination. I was unmarried (and therefore unoppressed) but I was lucky enough to have this man who was taking on half the housework.

The Arsenal group folded in 1979 and in the same year my partner and I separated, after nine years of an increasingly strained relationship. I was on my own, suddenly and truly on my own with two children. My life went into a dramatic reverse and I had no time for anything at all except work and holding things together. The girls were eight and four. It was a desperate time for me. Everything seemed on the point of collapse, though I did have another relationship, and very strong friendships with women. There was a fragmentation of people's lives. People were leaving London, changing jobs and things.

After that, for years I didn't go to meetings or get involved in anything. Now I'm in a group that's been going for three years or so. Five of us meet once a month. We read books by women, mostly novels. We also write, sometimes. I love it. In some ways it fuses everything that I find most important and rewarding about being with women. The first half of the group – we know very intimately what's going on in each other's lives – we talk about that, and then we talk about a book. None of us are academics, so there's nothing competitive about it. It's the notion that I think started with that Ruskin conference, that there's something about slightly ritualising, and regularising meetings, even ones which are based on close emotional ties, giving them a particular time and place and an interval between them, and possibly a task, that is not replaceable. It's taking the idea that friendship between women is essential, and actually doing something about it. That had everything to do with that Ruskin conference. However much I'd always felt myself to have friends and found it easy to make them, I could never have imagined thinking of doing that, of actually being in a group with women, before 1970.

Harriet recently went on her first abortion march completely on her own. I used to take her, of course, proudly display my womanhood with this baby. She doesn't particularly remember these marches. But this time she went on her own, and she came back and said, 'This is the most important day of my life, if I don't do anything else, this was fantastic. This makes it worthwhile. All those women.' And I was really glad. These were feelings that I remembered. That feeling of solidarity, a cause, of really affectionate liaising with people who you absolutely trusted and whose lives you were intimately bound up with. I really felt that coming together after Ruskin. It was something to do with the public statement – or public demonstration – of a private kind of closeness. I felt open to, and drawn to women, in a way I'd always been from childhood, but now felt it was validated. All those early feelings now made sense.

Juliet Mitchell

I have such fragmented memories of Ruskin. Visual images. I have this vision of these two women I knew. Thinking, good God, something has changed if people like that are actually coming to this conference. Grown-up intellectual women who had really been quite anti-feminist before then. They were all right, explicitly, they didn't need feminism, as it were. We had been seen slightly as hysterical making-a-fuss little girls. And yet here we had achieved something that they were coming to!

I was part of the planning group. Thousands of envelopes, literally. I was teaching English full time at Reading University. I stopped teaching at the end of 1970 because I was doing so much political organising that I was treating my job as a part-time job, and that's not fair to students. I was writing and organising. We'd got the London Women's Liberation Workshop going. *Shrew* was going by then. I can remember one woman speaking at Ruskin. She had that very feminine style, all she'd got for her talk were cards – and she had this habit that Americans have, they get up and say, 'I don't really know what it is I want to say' – and ten minutes later they'd say something. I got more and more irritated, it was so disorganised. Perhaps it was her anxiety, not knowing how to be together, seriously, politically just as women. It was very early days to have all-women groups. Those of us who had been in London for two or three years had got used to being among women and talking. But this was a huge event. Probably as a woman I had tried to charm a mixed audience. With all-women, the particular charm was inappropriate. We all have ways in which we use our narcissism to get an effect. I'm sure I did just as much as she did.

By then I had already been in a women's group for a while. Two of us were university educated, and didn't have children, and the others were the non-university women who did have children. We thought we'd try and do a paper together for the Ruskin conference with our university skills giving people confidence to write, and their experience of knowing what it was like to be a housewife. That was our contribution to the conference.

I'd grown up with a very proto-feminist mother – there wasn't a feminist organisation – but a single working parent. I had been to a co-educational school where there just simply was not a differentiation between what boys did and what girls did. A very egalitarian childhood, a wartime childhood. I was an absolute out-there-on-the-bombsite type of child. Very wild and rough. But also a lot of reading. It never occurred to me I wouldn't have a job. All of us had working mothers. Then I went to Oxford, where as a girl I was one in twelve of the student body. And one had this sudden extraordinary inverted pedestal treatment. Suddenly there was this huge difference between boys and girls, men and women, and it was sort of upside down. One was in constant demand, one was a privileged minority, but also considered inferior. Exceptional but inferior.

I had started writing a book about women in 1962, and it never got finished. The manuscript was stolen in Italy, and I had an incredible, traumatic reaction to its loss. We were travelling in a car and we parked in the Via Antonio Gramsci in Genoa, and our car was gutted, ransacked, and it had all our papers and books and everything in it. But to be fair to

108

the thieves, I'm not sure I'd have ever managed to finish that book anyway!

I was in this very male-dominated new left group that was dividing up the Third World into areas of specialism, saying, 'I'll do Algeria, I'll do Tanzania, I'll do Persia'. It was the beginning of a period of Marxist work which supplemented class analysis with considerations of ex-colonialism and Third World analysis. I said, 'Well, there's women who also don't fit into a class analysis. I'll do women.'

I don't think I would somehow have managed to finish the book anyhow, I'd got stuck with it, I don't think I knew what I was doing. I was quite pleased with the chapter I'd done on the suffragettes. The movement changed the need for that particular book. I must have lost the book in about 1963, I suppose. I wrote an article about women, 'The Longest Revolution' – it was published in *New Left Review* in 1966 – I wrote it in 1965, I think. At the time I was doing a Ph.D. on 'Childhood in the English Novel'. That's when I'd moved from Leeds to Reading. I'd gone back to being a postgraduate. Then I was teaching in Reading. So it was the first year of a new job. Reading was lovely. I felt much happier. We were a group of young staff at Reading, beginning a new sort of radical awareness other than either the old left or the new left. Coincidentally, I went to America the month 'The Longest Revolution' was published, to a Socialist Scholars' Conference. And there in the United States was the beginning of the women's movement. I immediately met lots of women who were beginning to think about feminism. I went to lecture on literature and Marxism, but in fact I ended up attending women's groups.

I was lecturing in Chicago on *Wuthering Heights*. I always felt identified with women novelists, and the whole question of heroines and girls growing up in the novel always interested me. Then there was the whole Laing and Cooper bit, the alternative psychiatry movement that became important in the sixties. We had got Ronnie Laing's first popular article published in *New Left Review* in the early sixties, I think. Through that we were all interested in the psychology of the family, phenomenological psychiatry. I used Laingian stuff in literary criticism, and of course I also taught about it in terms of girls growing up, and women being mothers.

I knew Sally Alexander and Anna Davin through the new left in Oxford. We all went back, you see, to some sort of connection: university, or some other sort of study group, or personal friendship. I should think we had about fifty people by then in London. Once a month, I think we all got together to plan Ruskin. Small groups met once a week, and once a month we had a London group. I think we might have been asked if we wanted to participate in the women and history workshop. In London we weren't thinking so much of it as a women's history conference, but more as a political organising conference to get women together. I think they'd had them in America by then.

Once I'd written the article in 1966 I stopped participating in the *New Left Review*. I was both pleased and angry with the way the article was treated in new left circles. Some of the younger people were marvellous, but one of the others wrote a response to it. I replied to that and I teased him about something he'd said in his response. He was one of the editors, and he changed what he had said after I had replied, so that the whole point of my reply was lost when the two were published. It was a trivial, final straw after a lot of tension, misery and conflict, and everyone's cross-relationships and affairs and God knows what, for years. It was the first article which had then been attacked in the magazine itself. I was in the United States at the time. I felt there shouldn't have been an attack in the first place – why pick this out as a first article to attack anyway? And then to falsify what the attack said so that my reply looked like nonsense. But that tiny detail compounded a whole history of personal mess. I'm sure the women's group saved the day as far as I'm concerned. It felt wonderful to have an alternative reference point.

I must say, though, there's never been a complete group replacement for the new left intellectual life. Not even within psychoanalysis. I miss something about it, yes, but whether that's missing also a particular historical epoch, I'm not sure. I think in the new left there were people who were really creative intellectually, and there were people who were just charlatans. I do miss the people who were really good. Raymond Williams. I felt terrible when he died. An enormous loss. A real person in our culture. I don't mean I used to talk to him every week, he was by then an older generation of the new left, but as a reference point, he was there. I called 'The Longest Revolution' after his book *The Long Revolution*. It was a small tribute to a heritage.

Ruskin gave me a sense of politics. I think the intellectualism of the new left was very apolitical. That's why a lot of people on the broader new left went into sectarian politics, once other radical movements like students had gone, people who were just in the new left realised they hadn't a political base and a lot of them became Trotskyist. The women who didn't become feminists had to go into sectarian groups, I think, just looking for a politics. Whereas those of us that went to Ruskin and started the women's movement had a politics. You may criticise the politics, but it was a politics. I think we tried to reach a unified overarching position. Today we celebrate multifarious political positions, that's the 1980s, whether it's cancers, diabetes, homosexualities, feminisms – we see everything as a plural. In 1970, at Ruskin, we felt we had one goal, we were unified. Yes, we had that.

You'd already got a division in America, between Marxist feminists and radical feminists, some of whom were radical socialists, but others of whom were quite radical right wing. Capitalist women. At that time, we didn't have that here. At the beginning in England you did feel you could have one feminism. One 'women's liberation'. I think we went on

111

calling it women's liberation in order to preserve the sense that it was an umbrella that could accommodate people of various left-wing radical politics.

It was an illusion, but you have to have those illusions to build a party, a political group. Looking back, I suppose we were laying claim to an innate psychism, something that all women shared. At the time it was happening it felt like politics, as the student movement did, and the Black movement did. We really were trying to understand why it was that women were in this position. We said a) that they *were* in that position, b) why were they in that position? c) let's do something about it. It doesn't mean it's a successful politics or a lasting politics. But I think the combination of a practice and an attempt at analysis, constitutes a politics. There was a conflict, a terrific conflict between the women and the men on the left. But there wasn't a conflict for women who were socialists. Not in my group. For us it was completely compatible to be feminist and socialist.

Audrey Battersby

I couldn't tell you how I heard about the first National Women's Conference in Oxford. There was just this amazing bush telegraph going on.

In 1967 I was living in Islington, on my own with three children, and going quietly crazy. I started fishing around for where to put myself politically, not really knowing what I was looking for. I had an interview with the chairman of the Socialist Labour League. He said, 'learn to type and learn to drive a car, and we'll have you'!

Then I heard about a course run by Juliet Mitchell, called something like 'The Role of Women in Society'. It was at the old Bertrand Russell Foundation building, just off Old Street roundabout. That really excited me because I don't think I'd ever thought about my role as a woman in society and that I actually had anything in common with other women. I had thought my condition, my disgruntlement if you like, with life and marriage and everything, was personal.

We always used to sit round the bar afterwards. An American woman came to talk to us about the women's movement in the United States, and said, 'Why haven't you got a women's movement here?' We just gaped at her. I think the big excuse for just feeling angry and not doing anything was that we were mothers with small children and there

113

wasn't any time. It was as a result of talking to other women – about child-rearing mostly – that we decided to have a series of meetings. Some fathers came, and, needless to say, dominated the proceedings. Somehow or other, people started connecting. More and more meetings started happening, most of them informally. By that time, I was fired up with some desire to do something, I didn't quite know what, but I knew it was to do with being female and being angry. I'd known my husband since I was about sixteen. The exciting thing for me about this period was that here were relationships which were totally independent of marriage, which were stimulating and interesting.

I remember one extraordinary woman who lived in Islington; big Vietnam flag painted all along one wall, it was a commune. She was the one who broke the windows of Selfridges. Something to do with smashing up cosmetic counters, and pinching men's bottoms on escalators. She was an activist militant, and she changed my ideas about my own femininity. It was beginning to dawn on me that feminism had a link with the suffragettes. I'd always been a socialist, anti-nuclear marcher, anti-apartheid, that sort of thing, but this was different because it was our own struggle.

One of the most visual memories of the Ruskin Conference was the busts all being covered up. The statues of men in the debating chamber were all draped with women's shawls. I think my first impression was amazement, at how organised the whole thing was. As we walked into that main hall there were people there with trestle tables set up, all sorts of publications to be handed out or for sale, and I thought, 'Who did this?' It was amazing. As far as I was concerned, it was very political. But I think some women who were actively involved in political groups like the Maoists were rather against 'women's lib', and wanted to make it much more militant. It was seen by some as a middle-class protest movement.

Having been a social worker, and then a mother, and

particularly a mother with a handicapped child and then being a single parent, I think the conference helped to gel all those thoughts and feelings and rages and whatever I had, and bring them into a kind of political perspective, which had never existed before. We talked so much, about patriarchy, child-rearing, the greater involvement of men in the family, ourselves and our relationships to each other. I know people go on almost *ad nauseam* – but that sense of sisterhood was so supportive and so powerful for me that it actually replaced everything I felt I didn't have at that time. We formed ourselves into consciousness-raising groups – my own group started in 1969 and we still meet, those of us who are left, twenty years later.

My socialism, which goes right back to university days, was totally male-dominated. I always took a back seat, I rarely said anything. I went, and did, and demonstrated and whatever, but I was still the little woman. So when I got involved in what I regarded as my own movement – and that was the exciting thing about it, it had got nothing to do with the men – I couldn't help but be upset when it started behaving like male-dominated politics and we started falling out over various issues. I was dreadfully upset by internal bickerings in the women's movement. But I think also, on another level, I knew that it was inevitable, that people were going to fight.

I think everybody was being carried forward on a kind of tidal wave, and it wasn't just to do with the women's movement, it was also to do with the late 1960s and early 1970s and what was going on at the time, worldwide. There was a surge of optimism towards radical change. And of course that has died down. I felt and experienced sisterhood amongst women in a way that I certainly didn't when I was younger. But then we were all more competitive in those days. I don't think I liked women so much when I was a young woman because we were so busy being competitive with each other for male attention.

After Ruskin I felt I had rights, of all kinds. Feeling also – and this particularly applies to women's politics – that it was important that we could stumble and grope around for our thoughts, our feelings, our ideas and not mind making idiots of ourselves, which I'd never been prepared to do before. Because it was separatist, I didn't feel so self-conscious. My whole attitude towards my sexuality, I think, changed quite dramatically at that time. I didn't feel like a sex object any more.

Whenever I cast my mind back over the women's movement, there's a sort of muddle of excitement and energy and ideas and meetings, but Ruskin was the beginning, for me. That's when it all became clear, in that great big conference chamber. It certainly was the moment of my becoming an active political animal rather than an inactive, passive one. I mean, I'd been going to study groups and God knows what, but I still didn't feel as though I knew what I was about, until I found my own cause.

I don't know how you can separate your own personal history from all of this. I had a history of difficult relationships with men. I needed to be on my own to gain independence, and confidence. I didn't know that until I discovered the women's movement, because I thought all I needed to do was find the right man, and it would be fine. But when other people were saying, 'We don't want men around, we've got stuff to talk about,' it actually excited me very much because I suddenly realised I was being freed from the need, which I was brought up with – my mother's kind of socialising of me was 'You've got to find a nice man to take care of you'. Not having men around also liberated me from wanting to be sexually attractive. Didn't have to think about it. Didn't have to please. I felt as though I'd grown six inches. I got tougher.

That didn't mean to say that I was going to give up relationships with men, but I certainly wanted to think about them with a bit of space. I prefer to have a relationship with a man than with a woman if it's a question of sex. But if somebody said to me 'OK, from this point on you're going to be stuck on a desert island and you can only choose one sex or the other', I'd choose women. I find women more interesting. In some ways I still can't relate to men, and this is where, I suppose, for me it's failed. I still find men – with a few notable exceptions – like creatures from another planet.

I think there are people who are genuinely psychologically and even physically homosexual, but quite a lot of women made a political decision to become gay as a kind of statement of their feelings about men – that they're no good and to have nothing to do with them. I always felt throughout, whatever my anti feelings about men were, that the women's movement was actually trying to change the state of play between men and women. I can remember once going to a benefit concert for 'Spare Rib' and the man I was with decided to come along. Men were still drifting in and out of those things before they actually learned that they were not wanted. I was hissed by a group of women that I didn't even know, and somebody leant forward and whispered in my ear, 'What are you doing with a wanker?' I can remember being quite upset by this, because here he was, really trying to be supportive. And I thought, this is not what the women's movement is about. I really felt, and still do, I suppose, that ultimately it's about improving relationships between the sexes.

My father was a lorry driver. He died when he was forty nine. My mother was a clerical officer in a trade union. My sister and I went to the local grammar. I think the school was a most powerful influence in my life. I think there's a little voice in my head that says, 'You're an upstart, you might let somebody down, and what's more you've got ideas above your station.' My parents were very pleased and proud that we both went to grammar school, but I think by the time it got to going to university, my mother certainly had withdrawn. I don't think she ever understood, quite. We were on our own.

117

Now I'm particularly pleased that my daughter is actually doing what I would have loved to do. She's trying to be an artist. That's what I wanted to do, and everybody said no, no, don't. Working-class girl like you, you've got to do something useful like be a nurse or a social worker. So I became a social worker.

The awareness of my need to be 'creative' totally vanished during that period of massive activity after Ruskin. I felt that I was doing it. What I experienced during that period, and it was quite a long time, was an enormous amount of energy. I've experienced that once or twice when I've been creative, that kind of 'I've done it' excitement, like having a baby, or painting, when I did paint.

By 1976 I was working as a student counsellor in further education, where there were many like-minded women on the staff. I actually went around the staffroom introducing myself as a newcomer, and suggested that we start a women's group there. Quite a lot of women came to the initial meeting, but there was that difficulty, that one inevitably has, of people unable to commit themselves once a week at a certain time. Somebody had got an evening class, somebody else had kids. It didn't carry on. But it was very interesting to see how women who'd never thought about feminism became feminists, and it started to inform everything that they did. I actually did a little teaching slot on women's studies, and it wasn't at that time even thought of as a topic of study as it is now. So I felt in a way that I'd done my bit for the women's movement, and to some extent I felt alienated from the mainstream of the women's movement because of the radical feminist dominance. I took my politics into my workplace. Apart from my regular meetings of women's groups where we discussed a lot of things, that was it. I'd run out of steam, I think, by then. Feminism became internalised in me, and I didn't have to think about it any more, it just was. I don't think you have to get out your reference book on women's liberation in order to decide how you're going to respond to a certain situation. I think it's got to be totally in you, gut.

Our group still meets. During the late 1970s we withdrew very much more into the personal, away from the political. You could moan, and you could talk about relationships, about feelings, worries. In a sense it became a kind of group therapy. I think it's had doldrums now for several years, but out of sheer loyalty and friendship we continue to meet. I think there is also a seed of optimism there that somehow or other it's all going to change again. I think there's been a lot of depression around, which has to do with the political climate outside, a sense that, God, we had all those ideas and all that energy and we didn't actually shift anything. Lives have shifted, yes. I think the initial ideas of the women's movement have taken root, yes, very firmly. But as for the socialist revolution, forget it. I think it must be awful for some of those old revolutionaries, getting to their eighties and still nothing's changed.

I feel I'm going to be like that one day. I think there are a lot of tough young teenage girls around who don't take the shit that we used to take. So there has been a degree of change. There is a very strong sense of sisterhood. Our group is rather like a bad marriage, in a way. But it's still there. Well, bad marriages can be very strong. There are times when I think, I want a divorce, and there are times when I think I want to shake this whole bloody thing up. But we're also very caring of each other and don't want to step on each other's corns. I look back at those heady, idealistic days and think, this is not good enough. But then I do get a certain satisfaction still from thinking, well, we did it. Created the climate.

Now I'm training to be an analytical psychotherapist. I've always been involved in the caring profession, so for me this feels like a natural progression. If I can be a good therapist, that would be very fulfilling at this point in my life. In a sense, it's all of those things rolled up into one: you can use

119

your knowledge and your intuition together and I think one can be quite creative actually helping people to change and grow.

This concept of creativity dangles over my head, all the time. I actually found myself saying to somebody on the telephone, 'If I could paint one half-decent picture, or write one half-decent poem, or – wait for it – have a baby (and I'm much too old) then I'd probably give up psychotherapy tomorrow.' Motherhood and caring – that's where my creativity went. I wanted to be able to do something well. I feel as though I've got near it a few times, but never quite to it. And this is why the written word, or the painted picture, for me is very potent. Why don't I take myself to the Camden Arts Centre and start doing life drawing classes? I am also, I have to tell you, quite lazy. The laziness is also to do with fear. Actually, I don't believe there's such a thing as laziness, I have patients who tell me they're lazy, and I don't accept that at all. I think they're blocked in some way, and I know I'm blocked in some way. I'm very frightened of failure.

Ruskin enabled me, for the very first time, to see women as powerful people. It made me think maybe I could be one of them. Women are more potent and powerful than most men, actually.

I think a lot of men have been affected by having to face up to changes in their women, and a lot of them weren't able to.

The women's movement has stopped me feeling that at fifty-odd it's time to put on the slippers and switch on the telly and stop thinking. If somebody asked me, off the top of my head, what's the most important influence in my life, I have to say the women's movement.

Marlene Hobsbawm

I went to Ruskin with a friend who was covering it for the *New Statesman*. I really just went along for the ride. I was a housewife. Full time, hundred per cent housewife. With two little children. A don's wife, in Clapham. I didn't go to university. I worked for the Food & Agriculture Organisation as a secretary in Rome. Then I got a job as welfare officer in the Congo, which meant looking after entertainment for the troops. Would you believe it! I think this must have been about 1960. I had to organise shows, films and football matches – things like refereeing a football match between Moroccans and Tunisians. Quite a chaotic year. Then I wanted to come back to England. The very first night I met E. I got a job with the Canadian Broadcasting Corporation at the BBC here, I was newsroom girl, using my languages, French, German, Italian – a sort of secretary, I suppose. Within a year we were married.

I was born in Vienna. Came here when I was five with my family, before Hitler. My father was very political. He already said in 1936, 'I don't want to bring up my family with Hitler as a neighbour.' So we came out nice and early, in 1937. That's how I speak German. My German is not good, I just understand it and speak *kinder Deutsch*, really. French – well, I was the first au pair girl, I'm sure I was. I'd never heard of

121

it before me. My father was in textiles, and he was a great one for languages, and he wanted me to learn proper French. So I went to Paris as an au pair for two years, and really got right into France and French culture, and Paris, and all that. Italy – well, I just loved Italy. I went there for a fortnight's holiday and stayed for 6 years. I always managed to fall on my feet, doing things that I could do.

We were quite comfortable. I grew up in Manchester. That's where I went to school. My father was the sort of person who always had his nose in the paper, and he was gloom and doom, as they were dancing the last waltz in Vienna. My parents were liberals, I suppose. You see, refugees were never very left wing. My father wouldn't ever let us laugh at the Queen at Christmas. Me and my brothers would fall about, and he wouldn't have it. This was the country that accepted us. We left Austria in style, with our cook, all the luggage, all my mother's cake tins. The cook doubled as a nanny. It was all frightfully bourgeois and comfortable. I myself wasn't conscious of being political until Italy. There was poverty, and the rich and poor there just hit you smack in the face.

E.'s mother also came from Vienna. So it did tie in really. And he always had his nose in the papers. He was another gloom and doom! I really launched myself into motherhood as nobody ever did. I was thirty, then. I did feel it was a very worthwhile full time job. People only have one childhood and one mother. I actually did some translation at home. (I took the piano up a bit, I had learnt in Manchester as a child.)

I read Betty Friedan's *The Feminine Mystique* in the 1960s, and remember something about women being frightened of going back to work, and therefore they had yet another child. I was sort of vaguely thinking what would I do when the children went to secondary school. But that's about as far as it went. It did strike me that it was a waste of time and stupid that one person was doing all this housework, especially as it was only for one family. And I did certainly feel that I'd never get out of this – somehow, somebody sneezed on the third floor but it affected you. Everything went via this switchboard which was oneself.

I had never been to a conference before as a participant. The one really big impression I had was that Ruskin was full of people who compared to me were already so liberated – I couldn't understand why they needed to be there. I was there by default, it was a treat, an offer, a free lift to another city, God knows what. But I was the one who really needed it! Whereas they seemed to me so young, so clever, so liberated. I thought, I'm the odd one out. It seemed to me I was the only real *hausfrau* there. My husband's job was to bring in the money, mine was to look after the house and the kids. There were a lot of young women with babies, who were fed more that day than in any of their whole lives. This was not every hour, this was every four minutes. You felt kind of naked *without* a baby suckling away.

They were all kids at university, with degrees, who were going out into the world, these young women had formed all their ideas. I don't think I was jealous. I just can't remember, whether I felt sad or envious or what I did feel. I don't know. I did feel excited. It was a wonderful day. The new thing, the new freedom. It did affect my brain, and I felt more alive than before. I mean, I was full of criticisms as well, certainly of feeding those poor little babies, I felt awful for them. The draughts, with the door being constantly opened. I think it was the first time I'd ever heard anybody talk about people in my situation. That was thrilling. What did a woman like me feel with two small children? It had never occurred to me that anybody would ever be remotely interested, other than my friends. I saw myself in a historical context for the first time, I suppose.

Actually, I never felt oppressed by men. I felt that my situation was different. Maybe because I'd married a very clever man. It couldn't ever really be fifty/fifty in our household. I could say, 'Right, you do half the washing up', but I could never write the other half of his notes. There wasn't anything I could do that would be remotely comparable.

We moved to North London around 1970. Then we went straight off to Latin America for six months. I always thought I would not work until the children were right at the end of primary school, when I could really go out for half the day and say, 'Look, if you need me, there's the phone.' While the children were at school, I got roped into helping with the school orchestra, and helping friends' children with their music. I got paid in chocolates or flowers, you know. Then I started to get very interested in doing it, and I went on education courses. I really loved those.

When we went to Latin America I took a recorder with me plus a tutor for my son, plus a little piano book of my own. A lot of the time I was alone in Peru with the two children, in a flat. I taught the eldest a little bit every day and he got on like a house on fire. When we came back, he had lessons and I just fell in love with all the music that he came home with. I started accompanying him on the piano. Then I joined a recorder class in the evening for myself. We were a real club, we lived for those evenings, and then started playing at each other's houses. I was the most unliberated of them all. The evening class was alright, but to go out socially in the evenings and play recorder with friends – I found that very difficult. Music was my liberation. And it did also tie in with my past. My brother was musical. He played both the piano and the recorder extremely well. But as he was classified as the musical one in our family, Mother didn't really notice that I was too. We all had piano lessons. I enrolled in the City Literary Institute and studied musicianship and harmony for three years. We had absolutely marvellous teachers.

I began teaching recorder in primary schools. My life really became a lot nicer. Also having my own money and my own world, and people who knew me, and didn't know who my husband was. I am still passionate about it, even after eighteen years. I love opening the world of music to children.

I used to go to New York quite a lot with E. and a friend of mine there went to a women's group. I always did feel it was quite artificial, these groups, discussing, because all my life I've always had close girlfriends. I would never have been able to survive without having a good lunch with a girlfriend and talking over problems with her – that's always been my therapy. I've always been a person who has talked to women and not men. I never talk to men, about feelings. I felt at one with my husband politically. I did not see women as the oppressed, compared to the oppression of poverty, of Latin America. I didn't need to go to a women's group, I felt I didn't need to go to a shrink. I could do it all myself.

Feminism has been a good thing – I think I've reaped all the benefits from it without contributing anything. I'm very conscious of the benefits. People are much much nicer to women. It's just not acceptable, no matter how great or famous your husband is, to be just a sidekick. I'm terrified of trends going back to the 'little woman', like these right-wing women in America. They say that if you're stronger than your husband you've got to efface yourself. Unbelievable.

I remember being in Italy. I wasn't a great beauty, but I was a good looker, and tall and big and bosomy. You could never go anywhere alone without men always being after you. Especially an English girl. That's just how it was. It was the plague of one's youth. I'm told by my Italian friends that this isn't so any more. Anyway, as I grow older, I go back to Italy and look at the same churches and sit in peace in Tuscany, and enjoy it. By the same token I would now go to the cinema by myself. I would go to a restaurant – to go to a restaurant by oneself was unheard of in my youth. I would even go alone to a pub now and not feel awkward. For a woman of my generation that is a kind of liberation.

Lois Graessle

As a teenager I worked as a journalist on my home-town newspaper in Jacksonville, Florida, and then went to Northwestern University outside Chicago, where I studied journalism. In American terms I had a fine career cut out for me. I had struggled against going into law, because all my family were in the law. Near the end of my time at university something snapped, which is actually relevant to what happened later in the women's movement. I was about twenty and I slept with the boyfriend I had at the time. I was raised in a very strict Southern Protestant background, Methodist. It was very important to me, very good. But it also had some very clear strictures about no sex before marriage. That's just how you were raised as a Southern girl in the fifties. When that happened, it was almost like either I had to get married, or else challenge everything I was brought up to believe.

The South at the time was quite a different culture. My Dad was a judge and my mother was very involved in the community, quite a liberal person. I went to Selma, Alabama for the civil rights march in 1964, and that was also a turning point for me. At university, I was involved with people who had a very passionate political commitment – a protégé of Herbert Marcuse's was there, an older working-class radical – and I was involved with him in running something that

126

was very pioneering, not to say radical for Northwestern, which was a symposium where we brought people together to consider topical issues; the year I co-chaired the speakers' committee, we focussed on sex and race.

I look back in embarrassment at how naively we handled the sex symposium, but it did signal the beginning of an awareness. It was almost like shedding a skin. There was a personal side to this too! I never had any confidence in my physical appearance, always being on the plump side. I always felt like an intellectual girl scout, that's how I characterised myself. I never really felt part of mainstream social life.

After university I set off for Europe, and what I really did was throw myself off the edge of my culture, because I had no return ticket, nothing. I simply went off on this Italian liner. I set off with friends but got off in England on my own. I hitched around the British Isles, and went to Paris and Geneva for a bit. I had applied and got a fellowship at Chapel Hill in North Carolina to go back for the next year and do a Ph.D. in Sociology. So, the next step, I was working in Geneva, and it was Christmas, and I was meant to be making arrangements to go to Germany and study German so I would be prepared to do my Ph.D. I picked up a copy of the *Herald Tribune* and there was a small ad that said 'Additional Person wanted to join mini bus travelling to India'. So I linked up with what turned out to be seven Australians going back home, and we travelled through the Middle East, Afghanistan, and took a couple of months doing that. I wasn't a hippie, because it had nothing to do with drugs. They were all very straight Australians who'd been working in England for a couple of years.

Then I met this man – my life has been riddled by men making quite an impact. I've always had a struggle about living my own independent life and then a man intervenes. Which is often a metaphor for something in me that's not attended to. This one I had met in Jerusalem, an American

127

who really was a wanderer, and he was working for a paper there at the time. He said very wise, philosophical things. Then he came across to India and I linked up with him again and he was going to get a job in Bombay helping in the film industry or something.

We went down to the docks in Bombay, and there was this Norwegian tanker that had just paid off two of its crew – one of whom was a woman stewardess, and a galley hand – and they were leaving that night, so they needed two hands. So I left all my luggage and everything except my typewriter in New Delhi, and thought how can I miss this – I must have been a sailor in a past life. Within twelve hours I'm on my way to what turned out to be Japan. I worked serving meals and doing the cleaning for all the officers. When we got to Japan I left the tanker to go back to the United States to do my Ph.D, and within a week of arriving I was maid of honour at my sister's wedding. So here I am wearing a full length satin dress after a year of a rucksack.

Three days before I started my Ph.D, a friend of mine who had cancer said, 'If you decide you can't do your Ph.D., do come, because I'd like to get cured of cancer and do some writing, and could do with your help.' What I realised in some instinctive way was that to put myself in a Ph.D. programme, after all that my wanderings had stirred up, would kill me. So I went to take care of her in Washington DC. She died, and I spent several months looking after her children. This was 1966. They had four children between the ages of six and fourteen.

Then I went and lived in a trailer in the woods in Florida trying ostensibly to write. At that time writing for me was a metaphor for trying to hold myself together; having let go of the Ph.D. and clear direction, I was quite disorientated. Then this man I had worked on the tanker with was back in England and wanted me to join him – but when I got off the plane in England in Easter 1967 I took one look and knew there wasn't a relationship there – the idea of him had simply

128

helped me break away from the hometown lover who had been waiting to marry me. All I can remember is my mother seeing me off in Jacksonville and saying to me, 'Lois Ellen, I hope you find what you're looking for.'

In England I worked as a journalist on an East London and Essex newspaper called *The Independent*, and I covered Stratford to Epping and Wanstead. I studied part time at the London School of Economics quite illicitly – I wasn't registered, I went to classes. Originally I had talked myself into a Masters degree at the School of Oriental and African Studies; they'd offered me a place because of the way I spoke about my experiences in India. But I was really floundering. Then I met a man who was at the time president of the West Indian Students Union, and that's important because it actually led me to the women's movement. I quit the newspaper job and got a secretarial job at University College as secretary to the 'Breakthrough to Literacy' programme. Nuffield had sponsored a literary programme out of which came one of the pioneering literacy schemes for children. Then I talked myself into a Masters degree in Latin American studies. I started living with this man, who was an Indian from Trinidad, and was very involved in community politics, and playground work in North Kensington. In February 1968, I met people he knew and he had friends come over, Janet Hadley and the man she was living with, and she mentioned that the next weekend there was this women's group meeting. The group of women that had come out of the Essex Festival, they were meeting in Tufnell Park. In 1968. Something rang a bell somewhere. The next week it was raining and Janet could not go to the meeting. I lived in Battersea and the meeting was in Tufnell Park. I got myself there. Something hit me immediately. I felt at home, familiar.

I can remember one of the subjects was the first sticker campaign on the London underground. I remember kneeling on the floor with somebody – she was very plump like me and had long flowing skirts on, which wasn't something I was familiar with, I still had jeans then – and I remember the physical feel of the room which was quite warm and friendly. It was just like I'd come home, in some sense. I was thinking up slogans, and where they would be printed and so on. One of them was 'You earn more as a real whore'. Another was 'This ad degrades women'.

The man I lived with had a son of maybe three or four at the time, and I remember taking him to meetings with me. I was very besotted with him. Also it was a way of validating me; I wasn't married and didn't have any children. I went stickering with another woman; we would meet at, say, five-thirty or six in the morning at Sloane Square underground station with our packets of these stickers. Plain white with very rough black printing on. We would get on the District Line and would ride along to Dagenham and beyond, getting off every once in a while and riding up and down the escalators putting stickers on the ads and trying not to get caught. Then we would come back and have breakfast. I also remember, there was another sticker that had been designed to put on men's briefcases, and we would also ride the underground – I can't believe it now when I tell people these stories – during the rush hour and very subtly either pat someone on the back as we were getting off, or put it on their briefcase and then slip off the train.

At the time we had endless debates about the media. As a journalist I had a foot in both camps. Many women felt we should not talk to journalists because they distorted things, but one of the things I had learned was that whenever there was something in the paper, however patronising its tone, what it did was give information to women. We used to get letters from little villages in rural Wales, and women would say 'In the *Mirror* today I saw a notice about this. What a relief it is, I felt I was crazy on my own here all these years.' So it made me less ideologically pure than I think a lot of people were.

Politics in the American South when I was growing up was

very different to the European, ideological political set-up. So I didn't have any of the analyses the other women seemed to. That women's group hit me partially, I think, because of the sisterhood, the experience of the group and the community of us. I did not feel bitter about men, and I felt ambivalent about those images of women, because if somebody whistled at me, I always felt flattered, because I always thought I was the kind of person nobody whistled at. Anyway, for another of our early actions, we decided to do a demonstration against Nelbarden swimwear, the ones who advertised on that long escalator at Holborn tube station. We had a big discussion. 'Miss Nelbarden Swimwear' was going to be at Dickens & Jones and we decided to stage a protest there.

We wrote a poem, and we were going to have a coffin, with a dummy, and the breasts were balloons, we were carrying something like that. We went up the escalator to the swimwear department and just stood there and chanted our poem, and then we were ushered away. Also I was involved in organising the first demonstration against the 'Miss World' contest in 1969. We drew all the banners at either Rosemary Johnson or Janet Hadley's bedsitter in Notting Hill. We put 'Miss-Begotten', and 'Miss-Understood' and 'Miss-Behaved' on sashes. We took a taxi to the Albert Hall, and I remember sitting in that taxi and all of a sudden making that transition from something that was very private to us in our small group, to thinking we're going to one of the major concert centres in the world, to something that's going to be on television all around the world. Anyway, we put these sashes and marched around and got a lot of attention. The next year we disrupted Bob Hope, who was compering the show. What really marked those early days was a lot of energy, a lot of fun, a lot of laughs.

In the first few months of 1969, those of us in what we now called the Women's Liberation Workshop, decided we needed a newsletter, so Janet Hadley and I composed the

131

first newsletter and I typed it in the basement at University College after hours. That was the first issue of *Shrew*.

I was one year through this degree in Latin American studies, which intellectually wasn't giving me what I wanted. I remember crossing Battersea Bridge and thinking, 'I'm not going to finish this degree.' I regret in some ways I did not do so, but the women's movement had become very central, so I went out and got myself on a printing course, and did a City and Guilds in offset printing, my theory being that we were likely to write things that no one else would print. As a result I wrote and/or printed the newsletter for a very long time.

One of the turning points in the Workshop, and then the women's movement in a sense, was when those who were much more into the interpersonal, psychological, the feeling and experiencing, and those who came much more from a location within the Marxist and left tradition in this country, began to be further apart. I remember a very crucial meeting, in a room above a pub in Portobello Road, and my finding that I couldn't understand the ideological points being made – there was something more personal for me, and the structure and strategy of people with a sectarian left tradition I couldn't relate to personally. I can remember one issue of *Shrew* where it was much more experiential and personal, more on the lines of 'the personal is political', and how threatening that was to some. I can remember writing an article in that notoriously provocative issue of *Shrew* about my feelings about the son of the man I was living with, and taking him to school and not being his mother, and people saying this was irrelevant.

I don't know how exactly we heard about the Ruskin conference itself, but I do remember we had a packed strategy and planning meeting in my flat in Battersea. I can't tell you anything about the content of what was said. My facts, what I remember, are how people got on together and what was going on underneath, not what was spoken about.

132

I just remember the feeling of all that, and an amazing sense of it.

After that first big women's conference at Ruskin College, I was under a lot of pressure to help to lead a national women's something, because I was one of the few people that all the factions trusted, I think because I listened to all of them and was reasonably good at helping people to find some kind of common ground; and because I didn't come from any left-wing tradition. I think what I did was really facilitate people working together, although I didn't think of it in that way at the time.

I don't know the process by which it came to pass that I was asked to chair the final session at Ruskin. As I say, I think it was all the groups involved felt that the one person they really trusted to do that without an axe to grind was me. It's interesting how it happened, because the session was quite loud and sometimes difficult and divisive. I can remember standing there and fielding queries and complaints and different factions, and yet out of that coming a few things on which we could agree, and the thing ending, with some sense of completion. Some sense of achievement that the whole thing didn't disintegrate. I suppose I had those skills of facilitating in embryo, skills which I have come to use a lot in my work since then.

I can remember having a state of acute culture shock being at Ruskin, because there were very well-organised, very worked-out political people, and thinking that we were innocents in the woods. Like, people were not listening to someone, shouting them down, having absolute party lines which you caucussed about beforehand. We were so used to working in these small supportive groups in London, that we were quite taken aback at the organisation and direction of some of the stronger militants. I also remember someone deciding that what we needed was a dildo as a symbol of something, and walking the streets of Oxford looking for a dildo. I just remember that sense of culture shock. That we'd

133

worked on a very democratic and feminine sense of values about sharing and democracy, and seeing how strongly those were divergent from many other groups. That difference between the more personal and the ideological was an issue that was welling up in the Workshop that eventually, I think, split it a lot.

I was still a novice in terms of the system, English culture certainly, but I remember going to meetings somewhere near Oxford Circus that involved trade-union women. It was quite an education for me, coming across different groups, the Socialist Workers Party, different Maoist groups – our autonomous Women's Liberation Workshop women had been quite shaken by things like someone going away and writing minutes of a meeting which were clearly manipulative rather than a true record of what had happened.

Although many of the women in the Workshop were also involved in other political groups, there was something about the autonomy of the Workshop that was really important. It was more women-affirming, rather than either male-bashing or ideologically-bound.

After the International Women's Day march in March 1971, I kind of faded away from the movement and the Workshop and went to work with teenage girls. I was working with groups of girls and West Indian boys at Clapham Junction and I became aware that there was a whole tradition of group work which we in the women's movement had been ignorant of. We had dismissed anything academic and to do with the past, and so had not been aware of this – though at the time maybe that was no bad thing. We damaged each other an awful lot in consciousness-raising groups – as well as ourselves – because we didn't know how to look at issues of power, and competition, at the shadow that is present in any group. What happened to me increasingly in the consciousness-raising groups was a sense of a loss of direction and purposefulness. I wasn't clear what the point was. I had belonged to a group in Battersea, and had also been in

134

Tufnell Park. I'm sure these groups marked a lot of my work since then, that sense of talking about experiences and listening, equally, and also the memory of what we did not know how to face and to say.

There are ways that help you face more what's happening. We didn't have ways of doing that, we had an ideological block to bad feelings. True sisterhood – which I experience much more now – true sisterhood comes when you actually face up to the ugly bits. We were very clear at that point that we didn't want to lose anybody. That whatever people's outside political involvements, this was something that needed some coherence.

I also belonged to Notting Hill women's group, and I remember a lot of ideological stuff about not wearing bras and make-up. Well, for me not to wear a bra would be very uncomfortable. I was sitting there with a friend of mine while one of these discussions was going on, and she had always suffered from very severe acne; her liberation was to have make-up that covered that up. So for me there was a process of de-dogmatization, in a way.

The Workshop ran out of my flat for a while, and then we had offices. I remember struggling to work out how we inducted new groups and supported them. I don't remember much about the planning process.

I can look back now at my time at university and see there beginning a slow shredding of the skin, and it being very hard to find a new one. I think that's what the women's movement probably touched in me. It was only some years later when a relationship broke up and I ended up in therapy that I saw why it had touched me so much, because it touched me as a woman. It was about the feminine, not only about being a woman, about something actually very interior, very feminine. But I was a journalist, I had a task-orientated background, I didn't understand any of this at the time.

After Ruskin we planned an International Women's Day

march and demonstration, a resurrection of an old celebration, in March 1971. I co-ordinated the planning group for the International Women's Day demonstration. The Maoists were happy to have me chair the National Co-ordinating Committee. If I look at it now, I guess I was actually very central in a lot of that, but not in the content of it. I wasn't there labouring for one policy or another. I was about how it unfolded. I actually made sure newsletters came out. There was a feeling that maybe there could be a national newspaper or a national organisation, and some pressure on me to think about doing that, but I felt it wasn't appropriate to have an American with an accent stage centre in the women's movement in this country.

So I took the chance to go and work with girls at Clapham Junction which is what we'd all been talking about, 'getting to working-class women'. The minute I did this and didn't go to meetings seven nights a week, I felt that everybody disappeared. I started one of the earliest self-defence groups for young women, and yet I found I was being attacked at the same time for not being in the Workshop's self-defence group. There was a split there. Some years later when I ended up in therapy, I got a very sharp letter from one of the women I had been so close to, saying that I used to care about the suffering of the world and clearly now I had written that all off. This was before she went into therapy!

The man I now live with, when he took early retirement, knew he wanted to move back to Derbyshire where he had once been based. It was a very difficult decision for me to leave London which had been my home for twenty years, but it's allowed me space for more writing. The move brought back all my feelings about coming to this country, starting over in a new culture and reminded me how foreign I am, although I am also very at home here now. I had chosen to leave journalism when I first came to England in order that I could actually actively be involved in doing life, not observing it.

I never thought I'd write anything again, and now I find that writing is more and more important to me. The book I wrote with a colleague on planning and teamwork is proving to be a successful and useful resource for people, and that is a relief and a surprise. Then I'm also finishing the life story of an eighty-nine-year-old friend of mine, and a book on work experience for teenagers, with my former job-share partner, and starting a book on our relationship to money with a woman who is an unusual financial consultant. All of this is quite a surprise to me.

I divide my time between Derbyshire and writing, and the team and organisation consultancy and training I do, work that has been clearly marked by my experience in the women's movement. It was really a training ground for me.

Amanda Sebestyen

Late 1969 I read an article in the *Sunday Times*: 'Third World War, Women versus Men'. It was all about 'these mad American women', and I thought, this is it, this is for me, where are the English ones?

I'd left university – York – with an English degree. I spent 1968 looking for some sort of direction. Lots of my men friends were in the International Socialists. I was always attracted to the anarchist strands. I remember saying to one of those guys in IS, 'But you're always so horrible about women,' and he said, 'Well, Amanda, we see it more as a physical need.' It was 'we see "it"', not "them".

I went to a private mixed day school in London, then a demonic boarding school where the headmistress was shut away in the end. Then Queen's College, Harley Street. My class was different from university friends of mine. I felt I really didn't have the right to be political, although I also knew I didn't like the sort of literary intelligentsia that were just interested in listening to poetry. In 1969 I went to the University of East Anglia to do Art History, and after six months of that I realised I couldn't become a career academic.

I was looking for a job, living in London mostly. I was at a party and two women were engrossed in a conversation about the abortion campaign. I went up to them in my see-through crochet mini dress, false eyelashes, lots of make-up,

138

and said, 'I want to know about women's liberation.' They just looked, and got on with their conversation. It was very cutting. One of them, a visitor from America, was very obviously not wearing a bra, which only a few people over here did then. My first taste of radical chic was when I joined the women's movement. IS wasn't like that, it was young men in donkey jackets. My male friends were in the front line, charging the American Embassy and getting blood all over their faces. Their photographs are now recycling on Channel Four television and in books. I was way behind, in a red velvet-collared coat from Wallis Shops, wondering what I was doing.

Even though I got rebuffs from the women's movement, it wasn't enough to drive me off. When I look back on myself I was a bit like a plant, I just grew towards the light. There were hundreds of things that disturbed me: for one thing, everybody was very closely and unquestionably identified with the left. People already seemed to belong to something much bigger than just us women. It didn't feel like starting something, it felt like joining something. One woman had armlets from her wrist to her elbow all covered in bells that she had brought back from Nepal – there were quite a few people like that, wonderful looking people. It was a bit like going back to school and wanting to make friends, and not really knowing how.

I remember that most of the speeches at Ruskin were nothing I could identify with as myself. There was a good speech from Audrey Wise about working women. Then there was a speech that was clapped, which was by the Peckham women. That was about real life, and I still remember the bit where this housewife has a fantasy that the whole thing is already done at 11 o'clock at night – all the housework for the next day. People were standing up and clapping, saying, 'At last, this is about our life,' but of course it wasn't about *my* life.

I most particularly remember an older, middle-aged

woman standing up, clearly a lesbian, saying, 'What we really need is an Equal Pay Act, or an Equal Opportunities Act passed in Parliament.' Utter silence. The meeting closed around her again, and people went on talking about what they wanted to talk about, which was how to be part of the revolutionary left. People would wander in and if they weren't clearly part of some group they would get frozen out. There was nothing conscious about it, there was nothing said. I was aware of these cliques. I didn't like that.

But there were already people saying very interesting things that stuck in my mind. I remember noticing after about six months of going to meetings that my address book had been full of men's addresses and now it was full of women's addresses. I was obviously networking all the time.

I suppose I felt a bit vulnerable, being younger. Lots of things that were happening I thought were ridiculous: Maoists disappearing through the swing doors at Ruskin to consult their leaders and then coming back again to make speeches. I was never a Leninist. I was always anti-authoritarian, basically. It was partly their emphasis on being working class and I didn't see how I could ever join, although later on I did work in a factory, which is something none of my friends in IS ever did. IS had a vitality, but not for me. I didn't like the recruiting, vanguarding, Trojan horse sort of thing, no.

At the very end of the conference the Situationists did their graffiti, 'End Penile Servitude' on the walls of Ruskin, and put out a pamphlet. I liked the pamphlet, but in the end it was nothing about men and women. They always had quotations from Bob Dylan. It seemed at first that the pamphlet was going to be about sexual antagonism, but in the end it was just about smashing the spectacle, that sort of thing. I was very torn about the graffiti, because I liked what they wrote, I thought it was witty. At the same time I didn't like the criminality of it. And we also all felt very aware of the cleaning women who would have to scrub it off.

140

I was an usherette in 1968 in Stratford on Avon, library assistant 1970–71 in Hackney. Then I started teaching part time in Further Education colleges. By that time I was pretty much fully involved with politics. I was giving remedial classes in literacy, English classes for immigrants.

I was in the first Women and Art History group for about two meetings. I remember writing a piece about Kenneth Clark and what was wrong with his book 'The Nude' and really enjoying myself. It wasn't ever published. I don't know if my father, a Hungarian, ever really thought women should go out to work at all, though his mother was a professional photographer. My mother always wanted me either to be a civil servant or a barrister, which were the jobs she would have liked to have. It never occurred to anyone that I could be a journalist. Or take political action. My family voted Labour, but that was about it.

I remember going on that first women's liberation march, on International Women's Day, in 1971. I loved it. But we were walking along the streets and we were shouting 'Out of the office, Out of the house, Out from under, Women Unite' – and it felt aggressive, and I didn't think the women we were shouting at were going to join us. I am still always shy about that stuff.

I underwrote the Women's Liberation Workshop with money I'd inherited. There was a fire in the office of the magazine downstairs and I was sued for it personally although it was not our fire. If there was any money needed I would hand it over, but sometimes it led me into situations where I felt very alone.

I felt the printed demands of the movement didn't express me. By 1971 I must have felt women's liberation was to do with men and women being able to be much more different than they'd ever been before, it was to do with androgyny. Certainly it was more to do with being quite soft and very open, than with this clenched fist, open-mouth, rather constructivist public face of left-wing strategy.

141

I became a radical feminist, then I became a separatist. We were squatting near Kings Cross and it was exciting. But a certain point came when I felt really too tired. I didn't feel anything I was good at – analysing and discussing things and being intellectual, helping write pamphlets – was helpful to anybody there.

I remember going into *Spare Rib* and it was very much more respectable and well-groomed than anything I was involved with by that time. I certainly wasn't against it like lots of people were. Some of my squatter friends put out a parody of it called *Spare Tit*.

In the mid-70s I was quite close to Italian feminists – the first generation of Italian feminists were all artists and art critics – and I would write reports on them and the art gallery they'd started, for *Spare Rib*.

There were several deaths in my family in the late 1970s and early 1980s – also I left *Spare Rib*; there were dreadful rows and a lot of us left at the same time. The row was over separatism, oddly enough, and I ended up on the opposite side to where I came in – very critical of how the separatist side behaved.

I worked on *Spare Rib* from 1977 to 1980. I enjoyed that though I had a lot of health difficulties. Then I decided I wanted to move away from just being a feminist writer, I wanted to write other things. It was difficult. I went round the world with the project of getting myself well and also looking for different kinds of work. I started on a nature cure diet which has helped, and I'm still on it.

In 1984 I started doing art reviews. It's very much translation, I find, writing about art. It's like putting something from one language into another. I particularly like writing about things from the past for an audience of people who don't have specialised knowledge. I think that the left or feminist literary or art critics often don't write in a way that I would personally want to write. I don't think I could become an academic.

I'd usually had a welcome from socialist feminists, and I've only got one friend left who's a radical feminist. But somehow I always thought of socialist feminism as a bit of an élite, and I did have a lot of bitterness against the male left. Lots of the things that were said in those days, either in socialist feminist history or in other things that socialist feminists were pioneering, I just thought were wrong. The analysis didn't allow for any real antagonism between women and men, it was all about class antagonisms really, and the main class antagonism was between working-class women and middle-class men.

Now there's been such a proliferation of cultural feminism, not in the sense that we used to mean it as separatism, but there's so much women's publishing. I sometimes get asked to write things for them. We're a gang now, aren't we? You get asked, you're on people's visiting lists, it's nice they still remember you. This is all about the 1980s and about being on the make, which was very much despised and disliked by me and lots of my radical feminist mates, but people settle down. There's nothing wrong in wanting work that's interesting, or enough money, or a relationship: sometimes I do find it very twee, that's all. For one thing I think a lot of feminist writing has become dominated by the market. It puts me in a very difficult position as a person who's trying to make a career myself writing reviews. I think in the old days it was possible to be quite hard hitting in your political criticism and still stay friends. But now, if you criticise somebody's work sharply, you're also threatening their livelihood. I'm asked to review feminist theory and I find I've lost friends. I wouldn't say I've made enemies, but there's a coolness. People find it difficult to connect the fact that I like them with the fact that I've written those particular things about their book. I feel more or less like I've tossed the ball over the net and now I'm waiting for something to come back, and I get hurt by silence. That's difficult. It's because the movement itself doesn't exist any more, apart from

143

networks of people writing letters to the *New Statesman* or whatever. All movements seem to have people of a particular age, and after a certain age people go off and do their private things. The last couple of years I haven't been going to meetings at all and the few meetings I've been to I've found very difficult to sit through. I've started going to talks at the Institute of Contemporary Arts – this is what middle age really means!

I was going to write a book about the history of the women's movement, years ago. But now I no longer have a burning sense of the righteousness of my own position, or the wrongness of everybody else, I've got no desire to debate that with anybody. I've got no polemical book about it inside me any more. And I don't think I could do a history book just for the love of getting the past straight.

I'd like to be rooted. We 1960s people have had a prolonged adolescence.

Anna Paczuska

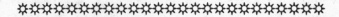

In 1970 I was in London after finishing college, at Durham. I was the first woman to study geology there. They didn't want to take me because they said a woman would never get a job as a geologist. They were half right, but it was the worst thing they could have said, because I then decided I wanted to be one. I'd never had any ambition to be a geologist before, and I didn't really stay with it long after. But that's what I did.

Then a friend of mine from college and I worked as labourers on the motorway, the A1(M). There were four women altogether, two of us from college, and two local women. There was a bit of a storm with the local unions, because of the high unemployment in the area. So we had to be on the basic union rate, which was fine, it was what we wanted, and we also could not work overtime. I think the *Daily Mirror* did a centre page spread on it: 'The girls working on England's motorways'.

I don't think I knew what a feminist was. What I did know was what my Mum had. She brought us up on her own, she had three daughters, and she was an immigrant to this country, from Poland, and she doesn't really speak very good English now and certainly didn't then – she used to say, 'Don't be like me. I haven't an education, I want all my girls to get an education and you'll never be dependent on a man.'

When I got married she was really pleased. She nagged at me because I hadn't ironed my husband's suit, but at the same time she wanted me to get educated and get a career for myself. It's very contradictory. My parents were divorced in the sixties. It was difficult in those days, especially with a low income. My mother had a terrible time. The priest came round and told her her soul would rot. She threw him out. She said, 'You never worried about whether my children had shoes, but you worry about my soul!' She's not so flamboyant now, but as a child I used to be really ashamed because she'd do things like, if she thought somebody was poor, she'd take them in and wash their hair and give them new clothes.

My parents came to Britain in 1947 with the free Polish forces from Italy. They didn't go back to Poland because of the change of regime. My Mum was deported to Russia during the Hitler-Stalin pact in 1939, when Hitler and Stalin agreed to carve up Poland between them. Half the population went one way and half went the other. My Mum went to Russia, where she spent three years on a collective farm, and building the Trans-Siberian railway. Then she and her sister and her mum came out in 1942 across the Caspian Sea to Persia. She met my Dad in Italy and that's where I was born. Then we came here. Travel – that's the story of her generation really.

My Mum hated rich people. Now it's more muted, I think she's got much more Tory. I think bitterness and disappoint- ment have changed her. But in the old days she hated people for being soft. She used to tell me that the richer people who were deported to Russia were the first to go, they were the people who died first of the cold. She had real contempt for them. She didn't have class politics in a kind of industrial working-class sense, she just thought you should be tough and self-reliant. She had contempt for people who had self pity and weren't prepared to fight to get on. She's always said anybody could be anything here. She refuses to see the bad things. She sees England as a land of opportunity, and that we've all done quite well.

When I got involved in left-wing politics at college, I once got on television being dragged off a pitch over a South African rugby team, and she wrote me a sad letter. She said, 'Is this what we've all struggled for, so that you become like one of those hooligans?' She always thought of the left as being pro-Russian, so for her it was me supporting the very things that made her family suffer. I don't think I've ever got it through to her that you can be a socialist and not support Russia. I grew up knowing that Russia wasn't socialist, that it wasn't egalitarian, and it was a nasty place. So I never had any truck with people like the Communist Party.

I think my politics came out of music and culture, really. Getting involved in jazz which meant being anti-racist. My first boyfriend was a jazz musician, and he used to tell me about racism. He was white, but he was really into jazz. I think being anti-racist came out of liking black music, which is quite strange in a community that didn't have any black people in it. We were living in Fareham on the south coast, just a small provincial town. It was partly that, and reading. I was best friends with a girl who had an older woman friend who was an artist, and she used to get books that I would never have seen. It doesn't sound very radical now, but reading Françoise Sagan and James Baldwin in a small provincial town in the early sixties was probably quite unusual.

Our politics weren't class politics, they were just radical rebel politics. You read, and you wanted to go out and do something outrageous. There was a local cafe where all the blokes with long hair used to sit round. And we used to listen to the juke box.

I went to Durham in 1965. It was such a snotty place. I was never so miserable in all my life. It's second class to Oxbridge, so it leans very heavily on tradition. Social life was a case of

147

getting invited to the college formal dances and getting invited to other people's colleges. That's how I perceived it. I may be wrong. Very middle class in its intake and very self-consciously upholding tradition. There was a belief in academia that wasn't borne out by anybody's intellectual curiosity. I expected university to be a place where people would be talking exciting ideas all the time. In fact I found people were ill-informed and quite poorly read.

The geology course was boring. I think that's why I got involved in politics. They used to have Socialist Society meetings on Saturday mornings, and they had rather a good magazine called *Durham Left*. Halfway through 1967 I began to go to the International Socialist meetings. I felt some sympathy with them because they brought out a pamphlet called 'Open Letter to the Party' which was a translation of a work by two Polish Socialists, Kuron and Modzielewski. It was a critique of east-European socialism, which they said isn't socialism and people hadn't got enough meat or other necessities. For the first time in my life I understood socialist writing from my own experience.

My mother was always a great critic of the Polish cultural revivalists in the *emigré* community. She used to say, 'We're in England now, we're English.' But I felt I didn't fit in. You got the feeling that at home people's mums and dads told them things that you didn't know. I can't explain it. It was just wonderful to read that socialist pamphlet, it did make a difference. I felt, here are people writing something about something I can understand and identify with, because it was about Poland.

What I knew about the politics of Poland were very much through family experience – the fact that letters were censored. I remember letters arriving from my grandparents with things cut out of them. When I was fourteen my father had a job with an English firm who got contracts putting boilers into power stations in Poland. We went a few times with him. I remember being appalled by the shortages of

148

things. People came up in the street saying could they buy the tights you were wearing. I found that profoundly shocking. I'd never really experienced poverty in the south of England. I knew there were poor children, and that some people were a lot wealthier than we were. In Poland I found myself going into shops where there were empty shelves. Sometimes suddenly, queues would appear from nowhere because there'd been a delivery of meat. That kind of poverty corrupted people's relationships with each other.

I joined the International Socialists in 1967. I had terrible battles with the concept of class. I think it's because of being immigrants, and my parents coming from a non-industrial background, I just didn't understand it at all. It didn't matter how many times people explained it to me, it made no sense in my head at all.

If you look back to old copies of *IS Journal* at that time the politics were open, very libertarian. Although there were people who had a very clear analysis at the centre of the organisation, there were lots of contributions from many different points of view. And of course there was the Vietnam campaign. The student movement was itself fantastically disparate and exciting. At Durham there was a small core of white South African *emigrés* so there was a lot of interest in things South African. We started a campaign to send back the South African rugby team from the Orange Free State when they toured. 1967, I think it was. We got up to Gateshead, and Newcastle University was playing the South Africans and we didn't know what to do, and this guy standing next to me said, 'Are you game for running on the pitch?' So we ran on the pitch. We didn't really know what we did it for, but we felt we couldn't sit there through the whole game watching the South Africans.

I remember we did a survey in the Durham villages, about attitudes to the Vietnam war. A lot of the villages were scheduled to have their services cut because there was no more work in the area, the pits had closed. I'd never seen industrial life in Britain. We were the only visitors they'd seen for weeks, because the bus service had been cut.'

When I was revising for my finals in 1968, I was in the house, and there was a knock on the door. It was a bloke and a woman, he had a big beard, like a Cuban revolutionary, and an Irish accent. He said, 'Are the International Socialists here?' I said, 'No, they're all on telly in Newcastle talking about the student revolution.' And he said, 'We're from Newton Aycliffe, and we're on strike for equal pay, and we wondered if there was anybody here to help us.' So we invited them in, and me and this guy from the zoology department, we thought, what do you do? You had to talk to them and sort out a line, and produce a leaflet. So we took them upstairs and sat down at the typewriter and we produced a leaflet, duplicated it and it was distributed on the picket line the next morning. Which upset some of the others, because they didn't mind going on telly to talk about revolution, but going out to Newton Aycliffe on a picket line at half past six in the morning was different! People grumbled and moaned, they weren't used to getting up at that time of the morning. I remember we took a football, and because we got there an hour early we played football in front of the factory.

The leaflet caused a storm in the local press. We said 'Women of Newton Aycliffe, the management is trying to make you work for less than you're worth.' That was my first experience of a strike and getting involved with workers in dispute. And women workers at that. As I remember it, it was the men who did the agitating for the equal pay. Most of the conversations were conducted in the pub, which was the place where the men and students go, but not necessarily the women workers.

I had one flash of feminism at university. They had a 'Best Dressed Woman in Durham' competition. The student newspaper ran it. I wrote a snotty letter, which they published, about, 'Is this what we come to university for? To be a mobile clothes hanger for some backwoods boutique?'

150

The other thing that was important, my first day at college we were given a really severe talk by the college principal, that we weren't to be caught having sex while we were at college, and that if we did we would be sent down. One student, a Danish girl, said, 'This is rubbish. I'm going to go down the town and organise myself a sex life, and then I can do some work at this university.' She wasn't rebellious, but very self-willed. She gave me a Danish edition of Simone de Beauvoir's *The Second Sex* in English! Which I never finished reading, but she said it would change my life, and it did. It made me think. It's quite powerfully intellectually feminist, though it's a bit dull in places. I kept it for years.

I got sacked from the motorway job for being cheeky to the ganger. We four women used to have tea with the men at quarter to four. But we knocked off at four o'clock. So it really meant that at quarter to four we took our tea break and cleaned up ready to go home. The ganger on our section had always allowed us to do that. A new ganger came on, and he said, 'No. The women aren't having tea with the men, it's not healthy. You can carry on working till four, you're paid till four. The men have a tea break because they work till six.' A lorry came, and I hailed the guy. I said 'Are you going into Durham?' He said he was, so I said, 'Right, girls,' and we put our shovels down and Annie and I got in. It was ten to four. We hung out of the window sticking our fingers up at the ganger. Of course all the men on the site were really laughing at the ganger. We got our cards in the post on the Monday morning.

I'd met a nice young man at the Durham Miners gala, I'd had a brief fling with him, and the next week he sent me a bunch of flowers, Interflora. The woman upstairs had sent them away because she said 'None of the girls in this house get flowers.' They came back a day later all withered. I was so taken. Nobody had ever sent me flowers before. On my way to Poland for a holiday that summer I stopped in London and I looked him up. He said, 'What are you doing when you come back from Poland?' I hadn't got a clue. He said, 'Well, come and live with me.' I said, 'Oh, that's a good idea.' When I got off the train from Poland three weeks later there he was. He had a flat for us, which was very enterprising. So I lived with him for nearly three years. Although he was very critical of many aspects of the women's movement, he knew I was interested and he always brought me home all the agitprop pamphlets, saying, 'There's another bit of nonsense from America.' I think that's how I found out about the Ruskin conference.

I worked as a geology lab assistant in a firm in South Kensington. Mowlem, a site surveying firm. Then I got a job as a research assistant at the Royal School of Mines, Imperial College. Jim worked for the IS print shop. To begin with it was only one machine in a printshop above the Tottenham football ground building. The rest of the print shop was a commercial concern which had a lot of women stitching soft porn magazines. The women would really object to us swearing, or saying 'fuck' or 'bloody', when we were wrapping 'Socialist Worker', and yet they'd be sitting there stitching up soft porn magazines! They saw absolutely nothing wrong with them at all.

The feminist movement took us by surprise, because when you're a student you don't realise you're different from men. You haven't got children, you're not in a domestic environment, you're very free. It's only when things like that impinge on you, you suddenly realise there is a difference and the world hasn't been planned for you. We started a discussion group in IS, the North London IS Women's Group. We said it was a way of getting women who had not done anything in the organisation for years to do things: 'Look at all the wives that come along here, and you've never got them to a meeting.' We got very defensive. Then we corrected ourselves, saying, no, that isn't the attitude, we should be actually for the women's movement because it's an important principle whether it gets us more members or not. Discussion was very fundamental, about things like the only jobs that women ever did in the IS was branch secretary.

I must have heard about Ruskin on the grapevine. I went with my mate Annie who I'd worked on the motorway with. I remember being absolutely overawed. There were two or three things I found staggering. The first was some women who came in shouting, 'Viva Solanas', with pop-guns going. I'd never seen women like this in my life. Where did they come from, who were they? I'd read Valerie Solanas's book, SCUM, Society for Cutting up Men, I thought it was hilarious. It deserves to be more widely read, and not too seriously. The other thing was, it was the first time in my life I met a gay woman who made a pass at me, which I found very confusing. I also met an old woman whose father had been on the Bolshevik Central Committee. I met so many exciting women, I can't remember who they all were now. People just came and talked to you. I also recognised there were lots and lots of IS women there. We had a tannoy announcement for IS women to meet in the lobby, and over thirty people turned up. We didn't realise that so many IS women were involved in women's liberation groups. We took names and addresses and agreed to keep in contact. It wasn't a proper meeting, we just met in the lobby.

I remember three speeches by people who were in the IS, one about the teachers' strike. I got up and said something about separatism in the craft unions, how women organising separately builds hostility to women from men, and how that can be damaging. I'd just read a book about the history of the print unions and what had happened there and why women were excluded from the print unions.

I'd always regarded men as the people I had intellectual conversations with. At political meetings there were mostly men, so it was men you had political debates with and discussions. Ruskin was really exciting, because there were lots and lots of women you were talking politics with. Nobody patronising you, you weren't out of your depth, you were saying lots of things together. I think that was very inspiring. Afterwards I just read and talked. Nobody would get excited reading Engels on the family now, but we did. We were on the phone every night to each other. It was purely cerebral. We just got into ideas as a result of the conference.

The speech that made the biggest impression on me was when they were having a debate about the relationship between women's liberation and socialism. There were speakers who said only socialism can liberate women, and then a speaker got up and said that's not true, look what goes on in Russia. We had a woman member in West London IS, she was married to an electrician, a really nice woman, Italian, she stood up, she had a strong Italian accent, and she tried to explain the theory of state capitalism, which was extremely brave of her. It did click to me then that there was a very obvious middle road, that you didn't have to be a separatist socialist or a separatist feminist, there was a very clear interconnection. For years I thought it was dead obvious, but now twenty years later I realise it isn't obvious. That current's all gone. It was very clear to me at the time – no liberation without socialism and no socialism without women's liberation. And it wasn't either admiring the Russians or admiring the Yankee imperialists or anything like that, it was an independent current which was about self-liberation. I just assumed, and I think we all did, that we could change socialist organisations into realising how vital that was. We were absolutely certain that it would be just a matter of years and everything would be solved.

We started a newsletter for IS women in 1972. We did it on our own money, it didn't cost the organisation anything. In some ways, while it was still a newsletter, it was more interesting, because we talked about the conflicts in the organisation. There'd be a heavy article about equal pay and why we've got to fight, and then there'd be a cross letter

154

from someone saying why wasn't there a creche at conference. I think we did 300 copies of the first issue. Later it became *Women's Voice*.

I was so busy I gave up working in geology, because of that. My boss said, 'That's the trouble, you go away at weekends, and you never go to conferences about work.' My boyfriend at the time said I was crazy to give up that job. I said, well they want me to spend my life going to conferences and flying round the world. I felt I couldn't even though I was very well paid.

I think also I got patronised, which was one of the reasons why I was so fed up. I was the only woman in the School of Mines. We were building a machine to simulate the squashing up of clays during the Alpine folding. This is of practical significance because it's about what happens to soils when they're loading and unloading, for instance in dam construction and motorway construction. It's not so much the Alps, it's what happens to new clay when you load it and how it fractures. So it was a well-funded project, which they found very hard to get anybody to run.

Not only was I a freak because I was a woman, I was a freak because of my politics. I remember an American professor being shown into my lab one day, and my boss saying, 'Have you met Anna? She's our departmental Trotskyist.' I could have thrown something at him. It was as if they managed to take all the seriousness out of my politics.

Later that year they all went off for their summer holidays, a lot of them were rather wealthy, colonial types, and they used to go skiing and water skiing and things, and they were all talking about their summer holidays and they said, 'And where are you going?' I said, 'Oh, I'm going factory-leafletting to Wuppertal,' thinking it was a hilarious joke, and they all believed me! So I thought, this has gone beyond a joke, I've got to get out of here. I left. I've been teaching ever since. I've never had an ambition to have a career really, so I just did what brought the money in. I teach maths and

155

computing now. I'm course tutor on a women-only computer course. I teach part time, because I've started writing at last.

I left London I think in 1971 or 1972. I went to live in Southampton. They had a very militant group of women in the Southampton IS branch, real fighters. We did a programme for Southern Television, and started a magazine called *Bread and Roses*. Initially the IS leadership didn't take us seriously. I think I had quite a schizoid attitude. I had a hard-line party attitude, you can't change the world without an organisation. If you don't have a working-class revolution you can't change the world. When I look back on it now, I wince. I think it probably got worse later on. You've got to join the party to change the world, because the class can't organise itself spontaneously. But my mates used to think I was OTT on women's liberation. I really enjoyed women's lib conferences. I went to all of them. To the bitter end. They were great fun. Even the last one, when I felt terribly alienated. I think it was because I turned up wearing a dress. I suddenly realised I was dressed all wrong. I know that sounds silly. You know how sometimes you're wearing the wrong thing. I wore a dress to Ruskin. And lots of eye make-up probably. But it was different then.

For the first three years I was married, I lived in Lancashire, and was very isolated. I was working full time. My husband was involved in several disputes. He worked in a GEC factory. I found it completely different building a relationship with women up there. I had a big row one night with some of the comrades in the IS branch, because I did a meeting about the family. A local convener, who'd been a member for two years, left the organisation after the meeting. He said, 'If that's what the socialists think about women, then I'm not staying in the organisation.' I know I hadn't said anything really freaky or way-out. It was mainly about how illogical the family was as an economic unit, how it's not really for us but for the state. It really upset him. I don't think in a London branch it would have caused that kind of row, even then.

I liked all the cultural side of the women's liberation movement, the painting, the music and the theatre. In fact, the last women's conference I remember I went to all the workshops on theatre. I'd only seen agitprop theatre and things done on the picket lines and on big demonstrations. I would say that I didn't read any fiction from the time that I went to college till probably some time in the mid-70s. I started reading again in the late 1970s, after I left the SWP. Now I devour three or four novels a week.

Women's Voice was dropped in the late 1970s, because the faction inside the Socialist Workers Party (which is what IS became in 1976) that had always opposed it, finally won. By the end, the editorial meetings were terrible, people were in tears. For a long time I was regarded as a safe hack that could be put up there and not say anything too wild about women's liberation to embarrass the organisation. Gradually as things tightened up even people like me found they were really alongside the fence.

Women's Voice as it developed, you see, became a magazine which was a women's liberation magazine. We talked about everything from menstruation and masturbation to women's history, to women's theatre. It wasn't an academic magazine, it was a popular magazine. By the late 1970s we couldn't organise round it any more because of what had happened to the women's movement at large, which was seen as the excuse to start running down the paper.

I think one of the big changing points was the end of the industrial militancy in the early 1970s. For a time the mainstream of the women's movement did actually straddle that thing between feminism and socialism. Every women's conference had delegations of working-class women. The Equal Pay Campaign united us just like the fight for the vote united women before. In the late 1970s the issue was abortion. Although socialist women, and NAC in particular, tried very hard to make it a class issue, it wasn't always clear. Equal pay is about your independence through work, so it was acceptable to women of very many outlooks.

I think the strains of the different factions within the movement didn't really show till the industrial militancy died down and the women's movement was thrown on to its own resources. I think that also happened in the SWP. I was driven out of the SWP in the end, after *Women's Voice* finally collapsed. We lost all the arguments. I remember one stage when somebody was attacking the concept of a women's paper. I said, 'Come on, even the Bolshevik party had a women's paper, it's not a thoroughly unrevolutionary unsocialist notion in our own history,' and this woman turned round and said, 'Oh, I didn't know the Bolsheviks had a women's paper, but it doesn't matter, it makes no difference to my general argument,' and she just carried straight on.

There are no basic tenets of the SWP in terms of things like their economic analysis that I disagree with. But I have very big doubts about the method of organisation, because I found it so personally alienating and I think the cost in terms of destruction of individuals is high. I never realised the price that people pay for standing up and sticking to things. For years women were such a powerful current inside the SWP and the IS. I never realised how awful it was to be defeated. We rode high for a long time. I never imagined that the tide would turn that far, that people would literally be driven out because you can't actually speak your politics any more.

One of the main reasons I never used to read fiction was because I spent every living, breathing minute in politics, and a lot of it was *Women's Voice* politics. Reading fiction coincided with coming out of politics. I'm writing now. Stories about Polish women in Britain. I don't know why they've come out like that. Some of them are whimsical. A lot of them are based on my family or characters in my family. Some of them are about situations, and I've created characters to carry off the situation. But they all have a heavily Polish thing about them.

I've got a granny who's ninety and never learnt English. She was in Russia during the revolution. She lives with my Mum now. I speak to her in Polish. Except it's getting worse. I couldn't speak English when I went to school. By the time I was fourteen I spoke very little Polish at home. I think a lot of early feminist fictions were moral tales. A little bit of passion is worth ninety times that. Something that people really feel. I like to think that my politics haven't changed, but when I'm saying all this to you I think I must have moved miles away from where I was twenty years ago. I wouldn't have dreamed of explaining a political insight like that then. I think sometimes disappointments are good for you, because you have to try and find something new to do.

Since Ruskin I've always thought of myself as a feminist, but when I listen to the women's group at college, where I work, or read women's movement literature now, my kind of feminism seems very different. Today's feminists would probably say I'm not a feminist at all, but I am. I'm just a different kind of feminist. I'm not a separatist, I'm a socialist feminist. I think the ideas about women's liberation and socialism that seemed so clear at Ruskin are the right ones. They may not seem right to women growing up today. My daughter often says I'm old fashioned. But when things start happening again, when workers start winning disputes again and women start fighting again instead of just talking, then I think the ideas will be revived and will be relevant and exciting as I found them then.

In the meantime you have to survive. I don't intend to do that by spouting old dogmas as if that will put the world right. It won't. You've got to keep thinking and you've got to keep being critical and you've got to keep believing change is possible. We're not dead. We're just waiting.

159

Val Charlton

1968 was a good year. My son Jud was born, and
there were all the Vietnam demonstrations. I was arrested
when I was pregnant. I didn't know it at the time, I was only
about three weeks. But I got badly kicked and spent the night
in Paddington police station with about eighty other people.
I think I joined the Communist Party that year. I was in it for
ten years, from 1968 to 1978. All our friends were in the
Communist Party, it was very much part of everything.

I was doing a teaching course, a postgraduate teaching
course at London University. I had done a Fine Art course at
Harrogate. Then I went down to London. I came from the
country. I didn't even know there was a Communist Party in
England, until I came to London. Most of the people around
were farmers, though my parents weren't. It was a very
apolitical sort of world. We had a cafe and filling station on
the A1. It was a very nice one, actually. We had a ballroom,
and a bar, and lots of dances there. It was the local dancehall.
I was a waitress when I was about thirteen, at weekends and
things. It was very isolated. We were not even in a village. I
was desperate to move out as soon as I could. I came to
London in 1965.

I didn't really want to teach, it was a manoeuvre to get
away. I actually taught for eight years, at evening institutes,

schools, all over the place. I had dozens of teaching jobs. London was very invigorating. I loved it. It was answering all the questions that I had when I was in Yorkshire. The big one that I hadn't understood was the question of class. I'd had all the responses to it without ever having any sort of analysis, until I got involved in politics. That was a very big personally liberating thing, in the way that feminism was later on. I went around with a group of people in the Young Communist League. Socially we went everywhere. We went to pubs on a Sunday night, where there was lots of music, singing and playing instruments. I really enjoyed all that. I was around for about three years before I actually joined. I didn't really do very much, I think I just went to branch meetings, and leafleted odd things, and just argued the toss. I also had some Cuban friends who were very important. They weren't in the Communist Party over here, but they were communists, and we lived with some people who were French-Canadian communists. There were also anarchists in the house that we lived in. So there was a lot of political chat the whole time. None of us had children. It was a very exciting time.

J. had been on all the CND stuff, as had his father. It was so ingrained in his family (his father fought in the Spanish Civil War), it was totally part of their life. So all the friends of their generation were also in the Communist Party. It just embodied everything really. I'd done quite a bit of sculpture. I stopped when I was doing so much teaching. I was making banners all the time, and placards and posters, and designing leaflets. I got pulled into all that, you see.

Before having the baby, I thought I'd just carry on working. I was so naive, I had no idea; it was a tremendous shock. It was all-embracing, when he was born, I reacted to it very badly. I really hated it; I loved him, but I hated the way of life. I was isolated, I was in the place by myself. I thought I was going insane. So I was very typical, I think, of people who were ripe for the women's movement. I think I'd been shocked by a difficult birth, and I was very shaky after that. I just remember that time as absolutely horrendous. Exhausted, confused, feeling absolutely terrible. I remember going up to Yorkshire, meeting a couple of friends of mine who also had children the same age, and saying, 'This is ridiculous, we can't live like this, we've got to do something about it.' That was just weeks before I heard about the women's liberation movement. I heard a group had just formed. Jud was a year old then. I went straight along.

I didn't feel at all comfortable. I thought they were terribly middle class. I'd been in the Communist Party, and the politics was sort of outside of oneself. I wasn't used to the personal stuff at all. I thought that was so indulgent, awful. There were a lot of Americans there, ever so confident. They weren't terribly warm. They were getting inundated with new people every week, so they weren't particularly inviting. They were a bit cool. I didn't feel very welcome at all. I went for six weeks, and then just thought I can't go on doing this, it wasn't what I expected. So I left, and got involved with other women in a nursery group, Camden Women's Action Group. We thought we had to do something, and not just talk about ourselves. I just hadn't understood 'the personal is political' at that stage.

Ruskin was just a few weeks after. The group that I was involved in by then decided to take a van up to Ruskin, and we all piled in somebody's dormobile. I was obsessed with it all. Totally. I suddenly realised that there were some terrible injustices to do with being female and having children. I thought it could be solved by a very practical solution, you see, by nurseries and support systems and things. I hadn't really understood the depth of the conditioning and the personal stuff. That took a lot longer.

I think we were just fascinated at Ruskin, sort of observers really. We were just goggle-eyed by it all. I had no idea there were so many people involved in it by then. They were very anarchistic looking, and a bit scary. I was much more

162

reserved at the time. There was lots of shouting, and writing stuff on walls, and people standing up and yelling at whoever was speaking. I'd never seen anything like this before. I remember hearing very very good speeches, by women. Somebody talking about women in prison, and an American girl talking about psychology. I remember being very impressed by the talks, thinking how can anyone be so articulate, so confident to stand up there and talk like that. I mean, I'd only been in London a few years then, so I was still very naive.

I had felt quite intimidated by the Communist Party – again I just hadn't come across such articulate confident people. I had been part of an arty lot from a little country town. We used to read a lot – but I hadn't encountered that type of person, and certainly not women like that. I think I was very intimidated by the Communist Party, by the politics, and I think when I first discovered the women's movement I was still trying to be a good Communist. I thought it meant organising, and doing practical things, setting up things. I don't think it's anything I'm naturally good at or interested in, but it was the only thing I knew at that time.

We talked about Ruskin for weeks afterwards. I think it had a very powerful effect. But I think we didn't really know what to say at that stage, we were still observing. I was reading everything I could lay my hands on. I can't remember individual conversations with people, but I do remember the impact of it. I was the only woman in my Communist Party branch, of about six people. We carried on valiantly trying to leaflet things now and again. They wanted me to continue because I was the only woman, so they supported women's liberation probably more than the main organisation of the Communist Party as such did.

They were quite nice local people. I went there for a number of years, once a fortnight or something. It was a very low-level activity. There was such a contrast between CP meetings that I went to out of a sense of duty and women's movement meetings which were bursting at the seams with energy, ideas, motivations. I learned a lot in those years. It took me quite a long time to have the guts to start criticising the Communist Party. Ultimately I got sick of the resistance of the men. It was ridiculous. We were having to fight people in the same organisation. This was after about eight or nine years. I'd done a good stint. I think we were trying to get them to take in the idea that the personal is political, and that what they did in their personal lives was significant, it wasn't just all out in the workplace. Also having women not being treated as sex objects in the organisation.

We formed a women's group in the Party, after Ruskin. There was a group of us who knew each other, got together and had meetings. We just happened to be in the Party. It was a lovely group, one of the nicest I was in. We did a big attack on the *Morning Star*. We'd written to them loads of times about using pin-ups in all their sports pictures, they always had pin-ups in white plastic boots and miniskirts holding footballs – we'd asked and asked them to stop it, and they didn't. So in the end we did a great big card and we cut out all the pictures of those girls posing – there was one particular photographer who was guilty of it. We laid it out like a big page in the newspaper, and we wrote a very coherent letter and asked them to print it. Of course they didn't print it, but the stuff stopped immediately. It was very effective. It caused absolute ructions. It was a very modest thing to do, but at the time it really shook up a lot of people.

In this group all the people were much more politically informed than in my first group. We met for about a year. It was a super group, it really covered a whole range of things. It changed all of us. We liked each other a lot. We felt we were part of the Party but we were also critical of it. I think that was the nucleus really, that started *Red Rag*. I can't remember whether the Party asked us to start a magazine, or whether we wanted to start it, and then they sort of collared it afterwards. I think the original women said they would start a magazine but it mustn't be controlled by the Communist Party. It had to be completely independent, and it had to involve people who weren't in the Party.

There was the most unholy fight about it. They hauled us up in front of their bloody committees. I remember one meeting where there were eight or nine of us, and one after the other said we thought it was unethical that we should be used by the Party to have a magazine. To gain the confidence of the women's movement we had to be there as individuals in our own right, not as a front for the Communist Party. We felt that very strongly. There were all sorts of accusations going round the women's movement about parties trying to muscle in. We didn't want to be in that category. The communist women genuinely saw the women's movement as something that could inform the Communist Party much more than the other way round. They couldn't see that. They thought we should knuckle down and do what they said. It got to the point where I think there were thirteen of us in one meeting, threatening to leave the Party. We would all hand in our cards. They were very rude, and very rough in the way they argued.

I started doing some more sculpture when Jud was a baby, and I did a load of stuff which I exhibited a bit in 1969–70. Then I suppose I just got overtaken by all the meetings and things. We'd sometimes go to ten meetings a week. The Communist Party, *Red Rag*, odd things for the National Women's Co-ordinating Committee. I was very involved with that in the early days. My address was used for that. Then the communist women's meetings. It was incredibly busy. It all got too much later on. I couldn't cope with it, and had to start pulling out, about 1974–5. I stayed with *Red Rag*, right up until just before it finished, the second to last issue, 1979 I think.

The problem with *Red Rag* – there were some communist women and some women who weren't communist, and there came a point where those two camps sort of divided. We went through various stages. There were times when we were very critical of the Party, and there were times when we actually got a bit defensive about it.

At first there was a lot of interest from the non-Party women in the Communist Party, and several people joined the Party. Then as time went on, I think we started getting more involved in the women's movement and more critical of the Party, and a lot of the non-Party women were actually getting much more interested in Party politics, and they accused us of not being – well, of being liberal, because the Party wasn't strong enough, it wasn't doing what it should have been doing, the Party was selling out – you know, the Party was the scapegoat for everything.

I never felt that the Party changed very much in its attitudes towards women, to be honest. I always felt the men made patronising token noises every now and again. They tolerated us, but I didn't really think they changed. That was why I ultimately left, out of total frustration and impatience with them. They weren't people I wanted to work with.

Feminism and the women's movement complemented the understanding of a class position. It helped me understand how I'd been formed. I saw myself always as being very much of an observer. That was a real nuisance because I found it chronically difficult to stand up and speak or take part in things. It's taken years and years to work my way out of it, if indeed I have – the effects of class and being female. I thought it was important that feminism had a class under-standing as well. That was one of the things that came up over and over again in the women's movement, the class antagonisms within the movement were constantly being tussled out. And then the race antagonisms. When we first started, we just had this big umbrella of sisterhood. I felt it and I know a lot of other people felt uncomfortable with all sorts of different types of people – but there was still the thing of sisterhood where you weren't supposed to feel it.

I found it very distressing to watch the thing almost

166

following the same patterns of other political organisations, where people just end up scratching each other's eyes out, because of differences; we hadn't found a way of co-existing. We were still trying to make everybody the same, still trying to say 'This is the model that we should all fit to'. Now, I don't believe you can do that. You have to have a way of looking at things which accommodates total diversity and difference. If you can't have that, you are just ruined from the beginning.

I think it's a dynamic situation, where you have to fight your way through the things that are the priorities. We cannot be allowed to discriminate against certain people because of their colour, sex, class, whatever. But having made those very basic huge general statements, we have to allow people to be very different. It's difficult in a society where differences have values attached and where competition rules. What sense is there in competition between people with different advantages; no wonder we are threatened by differences. Nevertheless we do each perceive the world from our own unique perspective which means we only see a bit of it and we need to collaborate with others in order to see more. It seemed then that everybody began hating the people that they didn't agree with; people were kicked out of groups – there was a terrible turnover in *Red Rag*. The minute a majority in the group decided that somebody wasn't on the right path, they were ostracised and chucked out, or they left. It happened so many times. It became ridiculous by the end, because if only two people had the right credentials to be in the group, there was something terribly wrong.

Maybe forty people passed through that group over the years. I think I really wanted *Red Rag* to let everyone say what they wanted to say. I wasn't too bothered by people saying things that I didn't agree with, necessarily. It seemed to me that the point was to show the range of opinion that was around, broadly on the socialist left.

I must say I enjoyed it, the graphic design side of *Red Rag*.

It was very important that the thing looked right. It wasn't any conscious style. It had to look competent and professional. It annoyed me if something looked messy and un-thought-out. I felt the visual side should be witty.

From 1972 I worked on films. I worked on *Monty Python and the Holy Grail*, and in 1975 I worked on *Jabberwocky*. I'd done some big films but I hadn't worked continually. I did special effects, building props and creatures and things that moved. I had my daughter Jessie in 1975. I left the Party in 1978, and J. left me in 1979. I was desperate to work. Professionally, properly; I was absolutely going berserk to have a proper career. I just sort of launched into special effects, and worked incredibly hard. I did *Time Bandits*, then *Dark Crystal*, *The Meaning of Life*, *Greystoke*, *Indiana Jones*, *Brazil*. Sometimes I'm given a drawing by somebody and I have to make the thing. Or sometimes I've been given a pretty free hand really, like with Terry Gilliam. He just tells me roughly what he wants and I get down and design the nitty gritty of it. Mainly it's been creatures and monsters. Anything that moves. Pure entertainment. I enjoy the making of the things. I don't enjoy the context of it at all. I think it's stupid. I think I work with some stupid people, notoriously right wing. I'd much prefer to work with people of a like mind. But they're just not there.

The women's movement was a fantastic training, really, because I came out of there much much clearer about what I was prepared to put up with from working with men. It's a pity more women aren't moving into those technical areas, because they need humanising. You need to be clear-minded, to not be conned by the way you get treated. The women's movement was phenomenal for all that. It must have sorted us all out, really, in a very powerful way. I notice it particu-larly with younger women coming in, that they don't have that really insightful way of seeing what's going on. I feel as if I can suss out a situation. I don't have to get angry any

168

more, I can actually see what people are up to, without getting too upset by it.

I don't know where the women's movement is at the moment. I have no idea. I haven't had anything to do with it for years. And the Communist Party for even longer. I've no idea.

I'm naturally apolitical. It was just that I hit upon a certain time. I loathe politics really, I hate political organisations, I hate the way those people talk to each other. But I can't deny they're important. I just don't like the type of struggle. I don't like people being nasty to each other. I fight very hard myself, but I don't like it. I don't ever really want to be involved in politics again. But it was a time of enormous growth and it's shaped everything I've done since and I wouldn't have missed it for anything.

Ruskin was very important, but I think it was so early for me that I probably didn't really appreciate exactly what was going on at the time. I just remember it as a tremendous shock seeing all these really wild people. It's the only way I can describe it. All the vitality and activity. It was only when I started living on my own and working and having to think very strategically about how I worked and survived with the kids and everything, that I began to feel centred.

I feel I've pulled certain things together, I know how to survive in my field, which is fairly narrow. I don't think I would have that feeling now had I not had that amazing experience in the women's movement.

What I'd love to do now is portraits, and have them moulded in bronze. That's my real passion. I do it at work, you see, I do images of people. I have to. Exact replicas of people for certain jobs. Or miniatures. I love doing that. I just think sculptured faces are the most incredible thing. They're the physical embodiment of the mind. You can see every thought they have, the way they think, their history – everything in their face. And yet they're all completely different. Like a language. I'd love to be an artist. I'd love it!

I gave it up in 1969 because I thought the contradictions were terrible, you couldn't make stuff and sell it to rich people and call it political. But now, I think if I could find a way of earning a living by just being an artist and doing heads, I'd be as happy as anything.

Catherine Hall

I was married in 1964, when I was nineteen. I was at Sussex University. S. went to Birmingham to start the Centre for Contemporary Cultural Studies in 1964, so we were travelling all the time between Birmingham and Sussex and it was very unsatisfactory. I was very unhappy at Sussex anyway, I hated it. You couldn't really do a proper history degree, because it was completely interdisciplinary. I'd been to a rather conventional single-sex girls grammar school, and the breaking of all the modes of work and so on which was part of the Sussex ethos I didn't greatly enjoy.

We got married and I transferred to Birmingham, and I finished my first degree, then started doing research. During all the student occupations in 1968, I was pregnant. Nobody else was pregnant or having children. It was really outside of student culture. That was one of the reasons why I got involved in feminist politics. To be a fully-fledged woman member of the student left at that point, you had to be around an awful lot, you had to be having relationships with X, Y and Z, you had to be part of the left scene. It's only in retrospect I understood that some of my feelings of marginality and dissatisfaction were to do with being a woman. I'm quite sure I didn't know that in 1968.

In December 1968 I had Becky, and it was a major trauma

171

in my life, absolutely major. I had no idea. I knew nothing about babies. I had no idea what effect it would have on my life. It really did break it up, pretty dramatically. It was completely accepted between us that I would look after the baby. He was incredibly involved and so on. There was never any question that we were going to share childcare half and half. I thought I'd be able to work while the baby was asleep. She went into the university nursery on a part-time basis quite early on. But of course, it turned out to be hopeless. I was doing research into the medieval aristocracy, and I never completed it. I had a grant for three years, and when I finished that I started working part time for the Open University, which started in 1970. That fitted very well, because that was either in the evenings or I could do things at home. I had this incredibly ambitious research project, and the gap between what I could do in terms of looking at documents and what I could make of them, and my aspirations to produce an amazing piece on aristocratic ideology and how it developed, was hopeless. So it wasn't satisfactory, and it was very isolated.

We moved into Moseley, which is a Victorian suburb about three miles from Birmingham University. I had to build a completely other and different life, and feminism was at the heart of that. Here I was, in my extremely nice Victorian semi-detached house, very isolated. I began to make connections with other women with babies. From the very beginning in Birmingham there was a strong presence of women with children. Two of us started the first group. We were both in the same situation, our children were within a month of each other. We didn't get material from the United States or London or anything before we actually started talking to each other. Just a lot of people at the same time were talking about the same things. We were nearly all middle class, and always dominated by women who'd had a university education. We were a classic group in that sense. Our first formal meeting was early in February 1970.

172

Then, either three or four of us went to Ruskin, and of course that gave it a great push forward. We were excited about it. At this stage it was still very unclear what Women's Liberation was. I can't remember where I stayed or anything. Hopeless. And there have been so many other conferences in Oxford since then, the memories are very inter-connected.

The last Women's Liberation conference was in Birmingham in 1978. It was a very unhappy experience. We put an enormous amount of effort into organising it. There were a lot of groups. There was always, from early on, a very strong socialist feminist presence in Birmingham, and there was also a strong grouping within that who were definitely in favour of national organisation and national conferences, and pushing towards more organised forms, really. I was part of that. We felt that consciousness-raising was as important as those sorts of political activities. There was potentially enormous power for the movement, if we could only mobilize it. A lot of organisation went into the 1978 conference. It just turned into the most hideous argument between socialist feminists and radical feminists. In the end it was so bitter and the recognition of differences so deep, that there hasn't been a national conference since.

The conflict was around sexuality, but it wasn't just lesbianism versus socialism. I think at previous conferences it had always been found possible in the end, despite the difficulties and the passion, always you could come back to some form of consensus about 'We're all women here together'. It simply wasn't possible to do that any more. I think it was partly that the kind of consensus politics which we'd managed to keep going, was extremely fragilely constructed – really there were an awful lot of divisions before the thing fell apart organisationally.

Of course, at Ruskin we had a consensus, at least for the four demands. A lot of women went to Ruskin never having been to a feminist meeting of any kind. At that stage I shouldn't think there were more than – what – half-a-dozen, a dozen, women's groups around the country. I remember seeing Juliet Mitchell in an amazing coat – do you remember the fashion for coats with fur collars, like Russian ones, with the fur running all down the front and round the bottom as well. Well, she had a coat like that. And blonde hair. She looked incredibly glamorous. I think I felt quite lost. It did feel like the beginnings of something. I knew a lot of the women involved in organising Ruskin through academic and new left connections. I only came to know them independently through the women's movement. I was also quite a bit younger than some of them.

I remember a huge room. There were galleries around. It felt as if some of the women there knew and had thought a lot more than we had. I think we felt a bit like young girls from the provinces. In the years that followed, I think it was terribly important that Birmingham was a big city, but it wasn't so big that it was fragmented as London was. We always maintained essential organisation, a newsletter, connections between groups. It was possible to keep a sense of the whole in Birmingham. It was very different from London.

Ruskin was different in feel from the later conferences. What I remember best is the big session, and the decision about the four demands. I think they helped us to shape what it was that we were talking about. When we went back, the most exciting thing about the next few months was the consciousness-raising. The first active thing we did was petitioning on South Africa – that connected us back into more traditional politics. There was always a terrible tension between the self-reflective and the active elements. One woman felt very critical that we didn't do enough campaigning, and that people wanted to spend far too much time talking about themselves. Some of the women in the early days didn't think of themselves as political, didn't define themselves as wanting to be involved in any kinds of campaigning activities, they wanted a friendship group where you talked about yourselves and your problems, and got

174

support. The first group as such probably only lasted about a year, and then we started lots of different offshoots doing different things.

I was in three consciousness-raising groups in the period I was in Birmingham, one of which lasted for about two years, until I left in 1981. That's over a period of ten years. The last one was very different from the first one, obviously. It was self-selected, and women who were all doing academic work, across Birmingham, Leamington and Coventry. We shared some common problems. In fact a lot of the other feminists in Birmingham were very cross, because they thought we were being self-indulgent. Elitist. We got absolutely done over, actually. We were publicly called to account. It was extremely stupid what we did, really. They were correct in their criticism. But we did it anyway.

We had a women's centre in Birmingham. There were constant crises about there not being enough support for the women's centre. You'd be energetically enthusiastic for six months or so, and then get worn out. Anyway, one such crisis, it was decided there was going to be a regular meeting on a Thursday or something, and at the very same moment that that was decided, we decided that this élite little consciousness-raising group was going to have its meeting on the Thursday. So the women's centre-based women were extremely cross with us and called a meeting to discuss it with us. They told us off, and were extremely heavy with us. It was a bad experience. Well, we didn't resolve it. We went on having our own meetings. They were quite right that that represented a move away from being willing to put so much time into the women's centre, that we were becoming more and more involved with being intellectuals.

I'd been politically involved since I was fourteen or so, in CND and the Labour Party. My father was a Baptist minister, a classical non-conformist radical sort of family. I have read the *New Statesman* since I was twelve. When I went to Sussex, I had a very bad experience politically, because Sussex

175

already in 1963 was dominated by Militant. It was awful. I had two other women friends at Sussex – in fact, that must have been the beginnings of the stirrings of my feminist conscience, because we were so badly treated by the men. The Militant men there basically thought they should get us to bed and then we would shut up and stop going on about CND. When that didn't work, then they just started denouncing us as petty bourgeois agitators. They were very hard line, and very nasty. So left politics became extremely difficult for me at that period. And then in Birmingham I got involved again through the student movement. But in none of those movements had I ever really felt that I was 100 per cent fully involved, committed, engaged.

The new feminism was about us. We not only belonged, we defined it. It was very heady. One of the things that was terribly important for me personally about feminism was that it absolutely wasn't my husband's world, it came to be my world. Coming to feel so confident in what I was doing and having my own space was extremely important in my relationship with him, and transforming that. He was a lot older than me, and he was already quite powerful politically when I first met him. Finding my independence in relation to him politically was a very important part of my growing up.

After Ruskin most of the time I was preoccupied with questions around feminism, for ten years really. It gradually became obvious to me that I'd got to shift what I was doing in terms of research. So then I started doing the work on the history of the housewife. Absolutely coming out of my own experience. One of the first things we did was to organise childcare co-operatives pretty soon after our first meetings. That was absolutely formative for me and wonderful. We looked after each other's children, but we always did it in small groups with – when they were very little – four or five of us, and we always had two women so that you weren't alone, so it was company and friendship as well. Just women.

One of the ironies about our relation to childcare was that at the very same time that we were madly criticising men for not taking their responsibilities seriously, we were absolutely claiming the sphere of children and home as ours and redefining it. Our house was constantly full of dozens of people and dozens of children and was very much my space. We were very controlling about wanting our power in that area, and actually excluding men. For a long long time, which was ironic. We built up a strong network in Moseley. It was a real community. Some of that has survived. There's still a women's liberation playgroup. Eventually we got a building. We spent all our time doing it. And of course I went to meetings every night. One of the things I've realised, working on the nineteenth century and so on, is the connections between what's often called separate spheres feminism, and what we were doing, building a power base in your own arena, your separate sphere. At the same time as loudly demanding equality, we were also insisting on difference. So that contradictory element was always there. Well, we were going to rule the world, you know. It wasn't just our nests we were ruling!

We had a strong sense of provincial independence. We made connections with other provincial groups, we weren't going to be dominated by London. Definitely not, I'm sure that was an element in it. One of the felt differences between us and London feminists was always a much stronger presence of women with children in Birmingham. From the beginning that was, if not the dominant element, certainly a very strong element. If you bring up your children together and those arrangements really last, of course it's terribly strong. You share so much and you rely on each other so much. The four women that I did that with, it survives in the sense that we're all still very close friends, and our children still know each other.

We had arrangements after school, because we were all working, so we could all have two late days a week. I think sometimes the kids had quite a hard time. It was complicated. It settled down to a group of three households and there were times when I think it would probably have been better for some of those children to be out of that system. But they couldn't be, because we were completely tied to it. One of the women first did teacher training, then she was teaching. Another of the women did postgraduate work, and so on. We all relied on it for our entry into the public world. In one household the man was quite heavily involved, because he was at home a lot. In the others the men were working fairly conventionally. They were very involved, in the sense that they picked up children, and cooked, and so on. But it was our system. We did it, we organised it, and we enjoyed all that. We were terribly pleased with ourselves. Lots of other networks were set up on the same lines. Baby groups, lunch groups.

I was at the 1971 women's liberation conference at Skegness. It was horrible. It left a sickening feeling. I was chairing one of the critical meetings. I remember I was wearing a stripey jumper, polo neck – I've always loved polo necks – sort of rust brown and cream. It wasn't that wonderful, I just remember it. I couldn't cope, really. It got terribly passionate, angry and tempestuous. Basically, the crunch was about whether a man could come into the meeting or not. The majority of us said he couldn't. But then there was a sort of physical fight about it. People were just screaming and yelling and throwing themselves around. It felt terribly out of control. It was only a tiny group, but the problem was when that was over, what could we possibly rescue from this ghastly mess?

The issue of exclusion of men wasn't minor, in the early days. I've noticed that in our literature, we made the point all the time of saying that most of our meetings exclude men and why we exclude men. We thought it was terribly different from anything anybody else had ever done. Actually it wasn't, but we didn't know any of the history of separate women's organisations at that stage. We thought we were doing it all for the first time. We didn't actually have to fight to keep men out in Birmingham. We had no Maoists in Birmingham. They were extremely vocal and strong at Skegness. They'd always worked out exactly what they were doing, they always caucussed clearly, and they knew what they wanted. Because of the notion that everybody had to be free to speak and we must all listen and so on, we had no ways of democratically voting out anybody like that. That was inconceivable. It upset us so much partly because of the whole idea that as women we were supposed to be building a movement together, and the notion of deep divisions within it was deeply upsetting. There were a lot of women who defined themselves as on the left, and who were terrified about left sectarianism coming into the women's movement. Which was of course what we were fighting about in those early days.

It did, it came in very successfully. That's why the socialist feminist conferences broke down, the last conference was just appalling, it was just one sectarian group after another. Those of us who were unaligned were desperately trying to make the socialist feminist current into something different. I certainly had a pluralist notion of the women's movement, and I never wanted the socialist feminist tendency to be split off and separate. But of course I did really want it to define what the most important issues were, because I wanted the women's movement to be a socialist movement. I thought we all ought to be working within the women's liberation movement more generally, but it was quite legitimate to meet and talk to the people who you felt politically closest to, to try and develop what you thought feminist politics should be about. It was always a struggle over defining the political ground. And the non-aligned socialist feminists, I always felt, were solidly within the women's movement, whereas the aligned ones usually came for instrumental reasons rather than because they were really feminists. They wanted the woman-power that we had and the clout that we had, but they didn't actually really sympathise with our politics. I think it took a long time to work all these things out. In Birmingham, the most active socialist feminists were all non-aligned.

I felt terribly strongly that I was a non-aligned socialist feminist, and I didn't want a party enough to drive me to join when I didn't actually agree with quite a bit of it. None of them put feminism first. The whole point about being a non-aligned socialist feminist was that socialism and feminism could be part and parcel of the same thing. That's never been true in the Communist Party or any of the others.

In 1975 I went to Essex to do an M.A., because there was an M.A. in Social History which included a paper on women's history. I did the M.A., and made the turnover to working on the nineteenth century, and while I was there Leonore Davidoff and I started working on a project together and eventually got some money. When I came to London in 1981 I'd become much more of an intellectual feminist than an activist feminist. Over a period of time I decided I wanted to work on the ways in which the middle class defines itself. We wrote a book called *Family Fortunes*, about the whole development of a self-determining middle-class culture and the central place of gender within that culture. Very much about the institutions and beliefs and practices of the middle class and how it is impossible to understand class outside of and separate from gender.

Then I thought that I wanted to do a series of different pieces on the middle class in relation to the Irish, the middle class in relation to the Jews, the middle class in relation to the Blacks, all in the mid-nineteenth century, which is the period I know. I decided to start working on the middle class and the Blacks. I started around the major debate and outrage in the 1860s when there was a rebellion in Jamaica, and it was very brutally put down and there was a huge public outcry. My husband is from Jamaica. We went there last

180

summer for the first time in a long time, and it was terribly important. The kids hadn't been since they were really quite small. It was quite shaking for them, and just brought up a whole lot of stuff about their identity. It made me think a lot about living between cultures and what that means. Basically I've realised that what I've got on to, looking at England and Jamaica, is just a huge and absolutely gripping, fascinating subject. So for the next however many years I'll occupy myself with that.

I'm terribly, solidly English in some ways. It's a very important part of my identity. English, but not part of the moral majority or anything like that. I only mean that I realise it would be very hard for me to live in another country. Living with S. has been a way of always having a relation to Englishness and being partly outside of it and therefore watching it all the time, and being aware of it in ways which I'm sure I wouldn't have been if I hadn't lived with a Black and had children who are Black.

My commitment to being a socialist long predated my commitment to being a feminist. Redefining that socialism became and is still where I think I am. Finding a form of socialist feminist politics.

The 1970s were a formative time for me – feminism helped me to think about myself as a mother, as someone actively involved in politics, as an intellectual. Amongst many other things. It's still crucial to my identity that I'm a feminist and my emotional life, my political life and my life in 'gainful employment' have all been shaped by this. I think perhaps our most important insight was that gender – meaning the social organisation of relations between the sexes, which always includes of course a power relation – is central to how society works and I'm sure that this is still far from being widely accepted. There is still so much work to do! But I'm not so certain about issues and rights and wrongs in the way that I was in the seventies – life, and ways of understanding it, seems to get more complicated rather than less so and the

181

absolutes of the seventies are no longer so clear. The optimism of those years has been badly battered but I remain convinced that we shifted the terms of debate in some ways that are here to stay.

Selma James

In 1970 I was an audio-typist working freelance for BBC Television mainly for the Current Affairs and Arts Departments, transcribing audio tapes of film which was then cut from my transcript.

I came to London in 1955 to marry a West Indian man, who had been deported by the McCarthy repression which swept the United States in the 1950s. The man I married was the leader of a political tendency within Trotskyism opposing the whole perspective and practice of the vanguard party. In the United States, I was a member of the minority he led. He had encouraged me in some work I began in 1949, on what was then called the 'Woman Question', and in 1952 I wrote a pamphlet called *A Woman's Place* at his urging. With the rise of this present women's movement, it has been republished in a number of countries. It's a very good pamphlet: my mother likes it!

I was born in Brooklyn, New York, in 1930. In the 1930s Brooklyn was a very political corner of the world. My family was part of that. My father had come as a teenage immigrant from what was then the Austro-Hungarian empire, what became Poland, and what would now be the Ukraine. I once tried to explain that to my schoolteacher when I was about six years old, but she was so anti-Semitic and anti-immigrant that she tried to make me feel like a fool. My mother's mother was Ukrainian Jewish and her father was born on a ship from Germany. She was American-born. She had married my father, an immigrant, to the fury of her entire family. She had run away to marry before the first sister had married, which was not done in the Jewish family. She had a reconciliation with her father on his deathbed.

Our whole community was framed by the immigrant experience, which gave me insight later on, about West Indians in Britain. Immigrant is immigrant. Immigrant working class is fundamentally the same the world over. As an immigrant you face similar problems of conflicts of generations, the racism of the indigenous population, and even the racism of other immigrant populations, against a background of ghetto slums and sweatshops.

I joined a Trotskyist youth group in 1945. It was the bomb, I think, and the period after World War II which, looking back, was a remarkable period of upheaval. In 1947 I got married and left home – because that was the only way you could leave home. A year later I was a mother. I was eighteen. I worked in factories and waitressing. My first husband was first generation American; working class, from Brooklyn. I met him in the Movement. It was natural for me to be in the Movement. I remember being about thirteen- or fourteen-years-old and telling my friend about how my parents had been divorced – which was a scandal in the thirties for working-class people, and Jewish people in particular – and that both of them had behaved badly, but that it wasn't their fault, and that when I grew up I was going to join an organisation to change the world.

I have always been fascinated by the relationships between people in the family. I'd been fostered out when my parents were divorced because my mother had to earn a living. I saw a lot of families, and they were all, in varying degrees, outrageous. I knew the difference between loving the family and loving the people within it. Kids know a lot, but nobody

184

asks them. When I was fifteen I looked around, and my sister was involved with this organisation. They read all these documents: I did not read. I never read a newspaper till I was in my twenties. But I heard, and watched, and said yes.

One issue was 'the independent validity of the Negro struggle'. It meant that Black people had a right to organise independently, and that what they said in their independent organisations had to take precedence over what the white-dominated working-class organisations were saying. I didn't know it then, but that was the Leninist view on the National Question. I read him later, and Lenin was just marvellous. He said, 'Scratch a Bolshevik and you find a Russian chauvinist'. As far as he was concerned, Bolsheviks were racists, against the autonomy of the nationalities. He had it right, I have no doubt. You don't need historical evidence (though there is plenty), all you have to do is look around. Even Londoners think they're better than anybody from outside. So imagine the vast Soviet Union, and these Bolsheviks in Moscow thinking they were born to rule.

The other issue was whether the working class in the United States was revolutionary, by which was meant not whether they were about to go to any barricades, but whether the potential was there; or whether working-class people in the United States had sold out for a refrigerator, which not everybody had even in England at that time. My political education began then.

I did all kinds of jobs. I worked in a factory packing marshmallows for a supermarket. That was one of the lowest paid jobs, and there were many Black women there. But in wiring and soldering television sets, there were no Black women except as cleaners. The hierarchy was so pronounced that even a relatively decent factory job would exclude Black women. I didn't think the union had anything to offer women, although I had been raised in the union, and I would have died to protect a union. But to attend the meetings as a

185

woman, no. I was trying to raise a family, trying to understand what was going on.

Then in 1953 my pamphlet, *A Woman's Place* was published, and I sold it in the factory where I worked. Women
liked it. People didn't think it was politics, although to me it
was revolutionary. But this was women, therefore it wasn't
politics. That taught me a lot. You could say a lot as a woman
about your private life. I never heard those things spoken
about again until the Oxford conference, and here were these
three houswives saying all the things that I had said in *A
Woman's Place* so many years before. It had never crossed my
mind that somebody else was going to say it. It was not mere
arrogance on my part to be surprised by the women from
Peckham. Of course women said these things all the time,
but privately, to each other. I had never heard anybody say
it in a formal framework. I was just thrilled, I didn't know
what to do. I thought, I must tell them. Then, no, that would
be arrogant to tell them. You must just listen. And I did. And
I was delighted. All of that charting of personal experience,
especially as a housewife, has since disappeared from the
women's movement, except in the Wages for Housework
campaign.

When I came here to marry my second husband I had no
money. I was not a financially independent person. I came
over with my son who was six years old. I was not a
professional woman, I was a woman who earned her living
by factory work. I taught myself to type, but I wasn't even
up to office level. When I was a child I'd made up my mind
that I was never going to work in an office. I didn't like the
way office women treated factory people, as though they
were a higher breed.

There was a state of emergency in Kenya – this was the
time of Mau Mau – and we were trying to get the foot of the
British government off the neck of Kenyan people, in particular publicising a teacher training school which a woman
named Njeri had formed despite the emergency. I was a

186

classical American ignoramus typing these letters to the Colonial Office. I didn't even read a newspaper. It was only when seven papers came into the house every morning that I began to look at one or two. I could not understand the editorials in *The Times*. I didn't know what they were talking about, even though I was articulate, and already had some experience as a public speaker. I was not without ideas. But I knew nothing of these 'world politics' or of convoluted sentences. And I was unfamiliar with British middle- and upper-class speech. I would pick up *The Times* and read it, and just did not understand. I thought I must be a bit stupid.

It was very cold for me. I'd come to London from California. I grew up in a slum area but we had central heating. I knew not to complain because I felt that's not the way to begin a new life. In any case, nothing could be done. But it was outrageous, when I think of it now. My son walked across Hampstead Heath to school. In a few weeks he had a British accent and asked me, 'Mummy, why do you talk so funny?' I soon learned how to be my husband's secretary, one of the things I was expected to do. But then I had a bad patch – being an immigrant is hell – and for a while I went back to doing the work that I'd done in the States: I got a job wiring and soldering in West London.

My husband was an educated European-style intellectual. I knew the words of popular songs, he knew the words of Shakespeare. There was a great difference. An enormous class gap. Popular music on the radio in England at that time was dreadful. They played operettas. I thought, what kind of a place is this? When I came to Britain I soon understood – though I might not have been able to spell it out – that the working class had no cultural power. The Beatles changed that. But before them, this country was very backward; the working class was considered beneath culture and creativity; only classical music was worthwhile; and the jazz aesthetes on the Third Programme kept well away from connecting the music they respected with re-evaluating or reversing their

187

stilted class or race views. I was terribly unhappy. Every immigrant is. But I recovered and I learnt how to live anywhere. I've never had trouble as an immigrant again.

English people were very kind to me. They had the most outrageous ideas about the United States. There was a nurse at this factory who asked me what an American was doing in a factory. I said, 'Who do you think produces things in the States?' She said, 'Oh that's right, it must be Americans.' She was a foreigner herself, some kind of European, I think, but she had the distinct idea that there was no working class in the United States. And I remember a woman at a bus stop on Haverstock Hill asking, 'Who are the servants in the United States, the Black people?' I was struck by her grasp. She was herself a servant. So I said, 'A lot of the time, yes. But white people are also servants.'

Britain was rigorously divided along class lines. My husband knew Fenner Brockway from the anti-colonial struggle in the 1930s, and Fenner showed me around Parliament. I could not understand why he was so proud of it. For me it was just another place where people were mucked over. I think there are some lovely places there, and I was deeply impressed by the chapel. It was really lovely. But I knew what governments were and I was not impressed. There was no way that I was going to find myself in a Labour Party which thought Parliament was wonderful.

We as political people were, among other things, in the business of trying to work out what people were actually doing and what lives they were actually leading. In the left you always analysed other people. It took the women's movement and the Black movement to challenge that. It took all the movements of the sixties really. Our phrase in the fifties to sum it up was, 'To record information about the new society'. You record the daily strivings of people for something new; that was a basic part of your job as a Marxist, to document the ways in which reality is not as the State says it is. And you can point to what you record of this subversive reality and say, yes, there is an alternative, and it is striving to emerge; here it is, this is the evidence.

In 1958 we were invited to Trinidad to be involved in the movement for national independence. Within a month I was entirely at home. I got a big education there. I learnt about West Indian politics and got some idea of what the issues were in Third World politics generally. Increasingly, I saw life from the point of view of a West Indian, and that has never changed. I saw the layer upon layer of racism. I was part of the struggle for independence and federation. I read and grappled with West Indian literature. I became deeply and profoundly identified with the Black and Third World political perspective. Not with any political party, but with the movement. I heard somebody say once a long time ago that it's not whether you're critical, it's critical from what point of view. I was critical, but accountable. I had adapted my political perspective to another experience. But I had not bent the spine, the principles, of my political perspective. It had only taken on an additional set of muscles and flesh. When you are committed to the end of the military-industrial complex, and you make another whole experience, that changes what you have thought and felt before, like a kaleidoscope. It absorbs what you have thought, and what you have thought absorbs it. They interpenetrate. Together they become something other than what your politics were before.

I had insights into my own background, by seeing other people's. Not as somebody other than yourself, but as yourself in other shoes. I don't know how to explain it really. I don't like the people who feel sorry for others or the guilt-trippers who ask you to. This is to assume that you and others are inevitably and forever divided from each other, when the point is to know that person is yourself. You don't cease to be the person you were, but you become another person – who you always were. Every other person has always potentially been you, but you have to discover and

189

bring out those other persons in yourself. You are everybody, every woman and every man and every child. The problem is to discover within yourself those others who have been put against you and who have been hidden from you or you have hidden from yourself – that's another complicated process. Politics as I've tried to live it is always enriching; it never robs you. Rather, it is discovering the world in yourself and using it to conquer more of what is hidden or mystified, in the world and in yourself. Learning. Growing is the only sound basis I know for changing the world and living a rewarding internal life.

We came back to London in 1962. There were many more Black people than when we left in 1958, a definite improvement. Europe had been so white in every way, not only the operettas on the Home Service, but even the way people walked in the street. Race ignorance and arrogance are endemic in Europe, but they have been challenged now.

I was immediately drawn in by someone, I can't remember who, to marches against the bomb. But I was careful not to get arrested. I had promised my son that I would not disrupt his schooling again. He got into a grammar school, and later became head boy. I was very proud. It was a tribute to the education he'd got in the West Indies and at home, but also to his character. I began to make friends who were quite independent of my husband's circle. I went on peace marches, but mainly I was involved on the question of race, going to court, standing bail, attending demonstrations, for the young Black men who were over and over persecuted by the police. But naturally I was closer to the women in the Black movement. I had always found myself with the women – those were my politics.

In 1969 I decided to visit the States. I was terrified because I assumed I was so backward: people said there was a women's movement, and I didn't even know what that was. I saw a lot of things that were new to me. People were taking drugs. I asked why, and they told me it was because they were programmed by their upbringing and this was a way to break the programming so they could choose how they wanted to live. I thought to myself, why can't they do it another way? It took me some years to find out that sometimes you can't. So the movement was knocking a little bit more of the repressive philistinism of the old left out of me – so capitalistic, really, in the sense that people are not ready to consider other ways of doing things, always laying down rules and conditions which have nothing to do with needs and principles, and everything to do with discipline – so you'll take orders and never be autonomous. Once you're part of the left, you have to guard against that kind of narrowness. I have a lot of it still, I'm sure. I only find out after I break from it.

The night I came back from my US trip, my friends met me and they said, 'You know, you've been talking about studying Marx,' and I said, 'Next August I will be forty, I want to learn how to read before I'm forty.' This woman said, 'If you're interested, I'm ready.' Seven people there said yes. We studied Volume I of *Capital* for a year and a half, and by the time I had studied for six or eight months I understood that the crucial question was women. There it was in the book. Marx's theory of value is based on the concept of labour power, and obviously what women do is produce this basic capitalist commodity. I thought everybody knew that, and they had neglected to tell me. I wanted now to explore this thing, to apply to women – not Marxism, but Marx, Volume I of *Capital*, the most brilliant, witty, wonderfully poetic book. A great political work of art.

I was breaking with a lot of concepts by the time the Ruskin conference came round – no, not breaking with, grappling with, wrestling with – 'Who are you in relation to the movement? Are you an observer? Is that what it means to be revolutionary?' And I was coming to the conclusion that merely to observe and analyse didn't even mean you were political – which would bring me into conflict with many

191

people. I had always felt that your politics and your ideas generally must be based on your feelings and perceptions; that you must struggle to find out and to face what they are, and on that basis come to your conclusions – even to the conclusion that your feelings are nonsense. No one thinks outside of their responses.

That is the positive and the negative; that's the problem, and that's the glory. The left has for many generations plonked a set of conclusions on reality, and they rarely review and re-work them. But most people really don't know what their assumptions are, especially political people, not in the sense I'm speaking of, yet they act on them. How do you find out what they are? How do you become what Marx calls self-conscious? What is a political organisation? How should it help you to become self-conscious? And how does it describe reality so that it leads to the appropriate kind of organising and so that you are not cut off from your constituents, the people you want to consider your reading of reality, and to organise with?

I was disappointed in what I saw of the women's movement in the States in 1969. The first group I met in Detroit crossed a picket line of welfare mothers that I had heard about and joined. I went to my first women's liberation meeting that night. A number of the women were social workers and they complained about how the leadership of the welfare mothers hadn't liaised with the social workers. I was outraged. They were complaining about the picket line they had crossed. How dare they! 'These are women who are struggling to get money from the US government in order to live. You call yourself a women's group, and you walked across their picket line? In Detroit?' – which has such a strong history of working-class organisation. Well, they looked upset, but the friend who had invited me, a woman who did factory work, smiled broadly. Women's liberation was a dilemma for her, in a similar way that it became for me. She was in a group with women who had usually shown contempt for women like her. Yet she wanted to be in a women's group, and there was no other kind then. They were all white. The welfare mothers were mainly Black. I said, 'It's your job to make contact with them, not the other way round. You're the ones whose job as social workers is to keep the money from them.' The social workers convened another meeting after that one and we worked out what they could do the next day. And they did it and were a help to the welfare mothers' battle.

I went to another women's group and they were discussing Virginia Woolf, who I didn't think much of. Again it was class; she had servants. But I read stuff, pamphlets, *The Myth of the Vaginal Orgasm*, and so on, some of which I thought had a bit of nonsense in it. (I still think so about this piece.) But the writings which were pouring out at that time (like *The Politics of Housework* and *Women Rap About Sex*), that was wonderful. I understood from it that there were other dimensions which we hadn't considered in the fifties. I came back to England really open to a women's movement, but cautious because my US experience had not been good.

A student at Ruskin, a close friend, a man, called me and said, 'They're having a women's conference here.' Then I got ill, and my friends said, 'You can't go.' I said, 'I'm going if I have to crawl. This is a women's conference. All my life I've been waiting for something like this.' I was sick as a dog, but I couldn't not go. I don't remember many things about the conference, only the feeling of it, the incident with the graffiti, my speaking, and the housewives from Peckham whom I later made a BBC television programme with.

I remember on the first morning sitting upstairs and hearing the Peckham women. I was deeply moved by them. Then I went downstairs to see if there was anybody I knew, and I began to comment to women I knew there, that I liked or didn't like this or that. I was very lefty arrogant. So they said, 'Why don't you speak?' But I hadn't come to speak. By

193

that time I was a practised speaker – I wasn't too scared and I was fluent.

I'd had to speak sometimes two or three times a week as organising secretary when we formed the Campaign Against Racial Discrimination in 1965. I'd decided then that I was going to get used to speaking; my mouth wasn't going to freeze when I tried to get the first sentence out, and I wasn't going to throw the household into chaos (which used to happen when I had a speaking engagement. I would see my husband signalling to my son, 'Let her go on'.) I was now able to speak without first having a nervous breakdown. Some people knew me as a speaker, especially on race, and as an activist in the Black Movement. A woman (now an MP) speaking for NJACWER (National Joint Action Committee for Women's Equal Rights) told us we had to 'join the working class'. I was annoyed. I'd never left the working class. Not only that, but I felt strongly that 'women's work' was a working-class issue, though I might not have been able to prove it then as I think I could now. Then another woman got up to speak about women in prison. She spoke about 'them' as bad girls who had to be helped back to her kind of righteousness and respectability. That really set me off. Since then, I've been a spokeswoman for the English Collective of Prostitutes. Truly the end is the beginning. I was furious enough to speak. The two or three women I was sitting with who'd been egging me on, were delighted. They wanted some fun, I think.

I remember two things that I said. One was that I rejected the idea that we had to join the working class: 'We *are* the working class.' The hall exploded. And I said, 'The Black movement has established that every Black person in prison is a political prisoner' – which most of those women didn't know anything about; I don't remember if there were any Black women in the hall. 'We must establish that every woman in prison is a political prisoner.' The women seemed delighted. To me that view was nothing startling. That's

194

where I came from. If you're imprisoned for stealing bread for your kids, who dares call you a criminal? That's how it seemed to me. But I'm not sure now how this was understood. When I finished there was this roar of excitement and people stood up and applauded. I doubt that this was a tribute to what I said. I suspect it was the right time for someone like myself who was obviously ready to break the mould which the speakers up to then were still within – except perhaps for Peckham. It was after all an academic conference, and academia has never left the establishment. And because there were so many women there, five times more than had been expected, I think, the power and therefore the expectation of the women was transformed. Oxford, organised as a conference, had in fact become a demonstration – which freaked out some of the organisers.

I was asked to speak at a workshop on white women with Black men. I remember only one thing the women raised, and my point of view on it. White women were worried that they were with Black men because they were Black. I remember that I was into telling them, 'When you are with white men you are with them because they're white. You are often – if not always – with people because of who they are in society generally. Even if you (mostly students on the way up) decide to be with people at the bottom, it may be because you want to tell your parents to go to hell.' The question of the hierarchy within society is never avoided; you're always choosing within it and hopefully against it, but not without it.

I was disturbed at the conference, but I was never able to verbalise until last year what precisely disturbed me. Most of the women were what you would call middle class or upper-middle class, and they attacked the lack of access of women to power. I always agreed, and the conference was a moment of power for all women. But still I sometimes felt funny when they were speaking. It began in fact at those two women's groups in Detroit, really, the one which referred to Virginia

Woolf as English feminism, and the one which crossed a picket line of Black welfare mothers. (I now adore Virginia Woolf, by the way. How wrong can you be. She's one of the finest writers I have ever read. Not the novels so much as her non-fiction. *Three Guineas* is a book for our time. Her approach is exactly the relationship that I was looking for between the way you feel and what you think.) After turning it over and over in my mind, and after seventeen years of collective discussion and campaigning, I understood that what bothered me then was the difference between being against injustice and being jealous of other people's power to perpetrate injustice. There's a lot of the latter in the women's movement, women angry with men for having the power they want. Virginia Woolf is so clear in *Three Guineas* about this. It's a political position, and it's also a personality characteristic, a way of relating to the world; the difference, for example, between self-expression – telling it like it is – and self-indulgence – not caring at whose expense you express yourself, which usually means at the expense of those with less power. It's a style; a nastiness, a vindictiveness, a jealousy and rivalry, against anyone whose power you want, including other women. What I'm saying may be obvious, but it took me a long time to figure out. Now under Thatcher – herself a classic careerist in a non-traditional job – we are seeing it full-blown. It is very frightening.

It's in the last few years, especially since Thatcher has come to power, that this careerism in the women's movement has become so conspicuous – has had the nerve to come out so stridently. The women's movement is of course much wider and deeper than ever it was, but this is only visible at moments and in patches. The feminists who are visible all the time and who are taken to be the movement, I've found on the whole that their concerns are not mine. In the twenty years since Ruskin the two elements of women's liberation have separated like curds and whey. They're interested in money and power for themselves. They're not interested in changing the world for all of us, in money and power for all of us, and that means that they are ultimately vulnerable and even amenable to Thatcherism.

When I came into the women's movement with that conference, I expected another kind of political discussion. I wanted to discuss women's relation to capital. What does the family do for the State? What are women doing against that family and the slavery it imposes? How should we respond? What is the relationship between the personal struggle and political organising, and how can we connect these? And what is the relationship between sex, race and class? A thousand questions I could ask – and that I and others have been working on since, and writing about and acting on.

I was in the Notting Hill women's group for years. We did a lot of good work, it was famous as an active and creative group. But I was never able to speak about my relationships with men, because I knew that women might seize the opportunity to slam Black men. They were lovely women, and they had much to recommend them. But one thing they almost all shared, and that was they were too frightened to oppose the State. If you are too frightened of bucking the State, you cannot get to the bottom of racism. A Black woman may or may not be very clear about men, white or Black, but if the police come after a Black man, she'll usually know what side she's on.

I don't like what feminists usually think about women who live more traditional lives and don't have the rhetoric to disguise this. Whether white or Black. I'm not too keen on the fact that they think that we should go out and get a job. I don't know what kind of job they think we're going to get, and who they think we're going to hire to take care of our children while we do that job. When you get to the question of housework, all that truth emerges. Mrs Thatcher is very clear: you do mine, and we'll both be doing a job outside the home. There was a lovely cartoon in *The Guardian* in January 1988: there's this executive woman at this big table – she's

197

white, and has a suit on – and this Black woman is cleaning the table, and the executive says, 'Isn't it nice, Mrs Mopps, that in spite of our different outlooks, we can both be equally feminist.' That's what feminism is now identified with; whether expressed in race, or class, or age, or whatever, feminists are identified as aspiring to be in management with men, and trading on their sex when they need to. Virginia Woolf saw this coming and in *Three Guineas* tried to head off what she called 'brain prostitution' by wages for housework: if women had money of their own, they could refuse to sell their minds.

The movement is always more than the individuals who claim to speak for it, and this women's movement is very big. At Oxford they sprayed the walls of buildings with 'Women in Labour Puts Capital in Power', something like that. I didn't think it was very clever to get the conference in trouble with the university, but I could see why they did it. I also remember how horrified some others were that women had put the backs up of Oxford dons. Tut-tut.

The Ruskin conference was very special to me. I met the women's movement there and my life was transformed. I think it was a massive learning experience, that conference. It helped to launch me into the politics that I've been involved in since. It focussed me. I don't know if it would have happened quite that way without that conference. The things that were established as positive at that conference, and in the groups that followed, that you work collectively, that each person has something to contribute, that the personal is political – my life is built on that – really collective, finding out how it's possible to give people who never speak the confidence to speak, without the group shrinking in size and scope. We found that if a woman can't speak, give her a thousand people to speak to and tell her to talk about her life as she lives it, and most of the time she'll do it brilliantly. In a small room, she might not have enough power to come out. Especially if she thinks that the women there aren't interested in her except as a specimen or a rival. In the Wages for Housework campaign we find this time and time again with grassroots women; they can speak like their lives depend on it, because they do.

Audrey Wise

In 1970 I was my union branch secretary, in USDAW. My father actually advised me to be very careful about taking a job like that, because it could tie you down too much. Being a Member of Parliament's different, because you retain a great deal of freedom of action, which is really important to me.

My work background was like a lot of women, married young, small children, just fitted in jobs mostly part time, shorthand typist, insurance agent, market research. Going-round-knocking-on-doors type jobs. Definitely not a career. I was eighteen when I got married. So it wasn't my job that was important in 1970, except insofar as my union membership was important to me. For a long time union activities dominated my life.

I joined USDAW when I got a job canvassing catalogues. They do it much more by mail shots now, but then you went round asking people if they would become agents for mail order companies. My husband had been victimised for his trade-union activities. We had a young baby. He was an active member of the Amalgamated Engineering Union (AEU), he was secretary of shop stewards in a very well organised factory in London. We moved away from London and he got a job in another factory, same sort of job, and in four days he was sacked. You get a reference and you think everything is fine, and you forget they've got telephones, and they know which are the organised factories. They see you come from an organised factory, and they're on the phone to your previous firm, and so on.

So I got a job canvassing these catalogues. There was this whole slice of my life, which includes 1970, when the union predominated over the Labour Party, and because of that I used to be invited to speak. I got sent as a delegate to this, that and the other. I was an avid collector of names and addresses, and I got involved in things to do with women right at the beginning.

The Ruskin conference is not the beginning. A lot of people think it was the beginning. But for me, the beginning of the actual feminist stirrings really was 1968. This is very important because it pre-dates the American influence. Obviously there was a lot of influence, and you're going to get interactions. But the first demonstration of women was in 1969, arising from the National Joint Action Campaign Committee for Women's Equal Rights. Every word was pondered in the title. I remember the discussions when we fixed the title. You could actually say 'NJACCWER', so you didn't have to remember each one. That was initiated by the Ford women.

There are two things that were so crucial about 1968. One is, it was the fiftieth anniversary of women getting the vote for the first time, not on equal terms with men, but for the first time, and that sparked off no end of articles – this sounds trivial but it wasn't – there were times when you couldn't open a paper without articles like 'Well, women have had the vote for fifty years, what difference had it made?' 'These mad suffragettes, why did they bother?' There was everything from that through to really serious evaluation. So a fifty-year anniversary is a bit special. That meant there was a kind of consciousness in the air.

The Ford women's strike was extraordinarily important, because it was the first strike since the match girls, eighty years before, which was identified as a women's strike. You had a Labour government which was supposed to be interested in equal pay and that heightened the consciousness as well. These women weren't actually striking for equal pay as such, they were really striking for equal recognition of skills. It was a strike which previsaged quite a lot of future discussion and argument. One of the things that gave it a heightened piquancy was the fact that it was very much a woman's job because they were sewing machinists. They were upholsterers. So when they struck – there wasn't all that many of them, I think from memory it was about 180 – it was in Dagenham, and the result was quite electrifying. They didn't really get support from their male colleagues at all. They got a certain amount of support from the union.

What is really central in my mind is the fact that they stopped the whole factory. Everybody thought of cars as being about the track, about engines, and metal, and here you had women working with soft materials, sewing, and they could stop a huge car factory. So it was an indication to those women and lots of other people of the power in their hands. Women are not used to feeling powerful, so it had a very great effect on them.

They didn't actually win. It wasn't until seventeen years later that they pretty well got what they first went on strike for. But they did make some improvements. At the time, the official AEU demand was for women to get the adult labourer's rate. You had about five grades in engineering, one to five, and then you had women. So the bottom grade was labourer, that was male. Then underneath you had women. And the official AEU claim which always made me see red, was not equal pay, not the rate for the job, not equal value, no permutation of that at all, it was that the minimum should be the adult male labourer's rate. Which would have meant an increase for women. It would have meant an increase for all the women in engineering. So some people thought that was a fine demand. But it wasn't; it was a profound insult, because it assumed that all women were unskilled and that the most you could aspire to was the wage of an unskilled man. It gave no recognition to the skills of women. I think there's a lot of rubbish talked about some work being unskilled. But that wasn't the point. The point was that men were graded. The grade might be imperfect, but the skills were recognised, and women, it was implied, had no skills worth recognising. At my trade union conferences I always spoke on wages, I never spoke on equal pay, never. That was a deliberate policy, because the equal pay debate was not seen as important.

I was in touch with the Ford women strikers. It's the sort of case now that goes to the Equal Opportunities Commission or the European Court or wherever. I was at the founding meeting of NJACCWER because I was in those sorts of circles. They realised that what they'd embarked on was something bigger than their own union or than the car factory, or anything. It was something which affected women in general. It sparked them; as always happens in a strike, people learned very fast. They wanted a 'National' organisation, and they wanted it 'Joint' to indicate that they didn't want to dominate, they wanted it to be all sorts of other women. 'Action' because obviously it was born through a strike. 'Campaign' in a way as a reiteration of the Action, but also to show that it wasn't just strikes, that you had to campaign in other ways. Committee for Women's Equal Rights. Very carefully *not* for Equal Pay, because they realised that it affected more than wages. It affected recognition, it was something in the head as well as in the pocket. There was a lot of discussion about that. That's how I remember the title so clearly, because of the discussion. There hadn't been a cross-union women's organisation, ever. This wasn't to replace any union, it was a campaigning body, to bring people together.

At that stage, there wasn't the feeling of 'women only' meetings, or anything. You did have meetings which were only women like women's sections in the Labour Party, but that was entirely different. They were a historical backwater at that time. This didn't intend to be an organisation that was just for women. Men could join it. Men did. In fact – this was something I never agreed with – the first secretary was a man. They felt it gave a sort of legitimacy. As long as women were in a majority.

NJACCWER will be remembered by quite a lot of trade-union workers. It organised a rally in Trafalgar Square. That was May 18th I think, 1969, before Ruskin was heard of or thought about. The first women's liberation demonstration in 1971 is usually referred to as being the first big demonstration after the suffragettes, and it just isn't true. It's quite important that it isn't true, because it's got to do with this idea that only middle-class women are interested in feminism. That's really why I make such a big thing of it if ever I get an opportunity.

We had a big rally at Trafalgar Square, and it was a pouring wet day, so there were all these umbrellas. On the platform, I spoke, the Ford women, perhaps two of them, and there was an AEU shop steward from Rolls Royce I think, Glasgow, who was a very well-known woman trade-unionist. And one or two men, the Assistant General Secretary of the AEU. I'd been on lots of demonstrations, and this was the first time I'd spoken in Trafalgar Square. I always regarded them as times when you met people you hadn't seen for a long time, and you talked. The last thing you did was take any notice of the platform.

It was very interesting to me that it was clear that these were women who weren't accustomed to going on rallies, because they drank in every word. It was a terrible responsibility speaking. These women on this wet day, and them tipping their umbrellas back a bit so they could see you, and you could see them, and they were drinking in every word. I thought of all the Sunday dinners gone uncooked. They came from all over the country. It was a considerable achievement.

Later on, some years later, I met some women from the Potteries, and they said, 'Oh, that rally, it was great, that was what made us really think.' Of course the discussion centred on equal pay, but as with everything to do with women, it can never stay on wages, there's no boundaries ever. I could imagine the conversations going on in people's houses – 'I'm going to London, how can we afford it? What about the dinner, who will look after the children?' Whereas a man would simply say, 'I'm going on a demonstration.' Full stop.

I met my husband in politics, and he knew what he was getting. He wanted me in Parliament before I did. I was the one who was nervous about being away from home and thought I would hate Parliament and everybody in it. In our marriage we've had a very strong concept of turns each, that we respect each other and each other's contribution. The big test of a man and his view about equality isn't whether he will allow you to go to equal meetings with him, it's what if you get to be the one who has the national responsibility? And that was the test my husband passed with flying colours. It's been a combination of luck and good judgement! But I recognise that.

There wasn't a women's movement when I grew up in Newcastle-on-Tyne, so I made the judgement that seemed good to me, which was that I would 'live equality'. I managed that. I'm very lucky in my family, I'm very lucky in my husband, and so I've always lived equality, and I've had men around me, my father, my son and my husband, who also agreed with that style. I took part in everything on equal terms. My daughter is now a fourth generation active socialist. I got it from my grandmother as well. She was a very early teacher of mine. I've had great difficulty with the designation 'chair' and 'chairperson', because my grandma, she taught me that the designation was 'Madam Chairman'. She would never have 'Mr Chairman'. She always would have it that you could be a 'Madam Chairman'. So I grew up with a model of women who did things. But my observation was that as soon as you've labelled anything 'woman' whether it was to do with pay or whatever, it was relegated. I might speak about low pay in women's wages and so on, but always in the general context. Everybody was in for the wages debate, but they went out for the equal pay debate. I was always a feminist before there was a women's movement. I used to regret missing the suffragettes, and then I decided it was a jolly good job because I don't know whether I could have been a suffragette! They were so incredibly brave. I asked my grandma why she wasn't a suffragette, and she wasn't because she was a socialist primarily.

I was invited to go to Ruskin. I didn't just arrive out of the blue. I imagine I was probably asked to speak on 'Women and Trade Unions'. Some title like that. To be candid, the title wouldn't have mattered much to me, because I would say what I felt ought to be said. I got this letter saying would I present a paper. I was totally thrown by this. Present a paper? I didn't present papers. I spoke. What were they on about? It wasn't my first contact with the middle-class background. Anyway, I got this thing saying would I present a paper, and would I bring four hundred copies with me. Well, a) I didn't know how to present a paper, b) how could I bring four hundred copies? I didn't have facilities. So I thought it was an error, and they'd meant forty. So I wrote something – I just wrote it, like what I call a piece, I'd written what I call a piece intermittently since I was fifteen, just for myself. I suppose what other people would call a paper. But papers are university-type things. It wasn't an article because it wasn't for publication. I just wrote.

I remember writing one when I was fifteen on 'The Double-Edged Nature of Education': obviously you wanted education – I was very close to my grandfather who left school when he was eleven and he was entirely self-educated – so I felt in a direct line with the Victorian working class for whom education was a tremendous prize. At the same time, I could see people buying what I then already thought was the gutter

206

press. So I realised you could use literacy in different ways. But you had to have it. As soon as you got it, they started taking it off you, by using it to brainwash you.

I managed to get access to a duplicator and did forty copies of this thing. Then in fact there was this huge hall filled with women! I realised four hundred had been an understatement. It was billed as the Women's Liberation Conference, and I was very uneasy with any of the terms. I just don't think we've got a satisfactory way of describing what we want. I don't like 'emancipation'. I don't like 'equality' because in some ways I'm superior, and all women are. I don't like anything that implies that you've got to prove we are equal. I think you're equal from the minute you're born. You haven't got to prove anything to anybody.

Early on I was saying, 'Don't accept the male norm'. One of the pitfalls that can be used as an illustration is women smoking. When I was a little girl women didn't smoke. Some did, and it was all rather bold. I suppose smoking then probably was an expression of 'We're equal, we do what we like'. And what a trap, because they've accepted some stupid habit of men. So, I've always felt it isn't a matter of getting equal to anybody. But 'liberation' struck me as a bit high-flown. Suppose I was in South Africa. Now there 'liberation' would be the word. I couldn't really see that it was liberation these quite highly-educated women in Oxford needed. They had a lot of liberty already, they had to learn how to use it. We've got a lot of deprivations, all women, and I don't resent women with a middle-class background. I don't care about background. Undoubtedly middle-class women have always had deprivations. The women who struggled for higher education, for instance, I always respected them very much. I think I prefer the term 'women's movement'. That's my sort of term.

I'd read Simone de Beauvoir's book, *The Second Sex*, by then. She was a real turn-off for me. In her book it was as though all men were privileged, and all women were oppressed, in a very undifferentiated way. I just could not accept this. At Ruskin, I felt I should be in a way a bit of a dose of cold water, because there was, I thought, a lack of appreciation of some of the worst of the deprivations that women had. So I wanted to inject the working-class thing into this.

If you're middle class, men have jobs like solicitors, they mix with people and they exercise a certain amount of power in their work. For the men that I was accustomed to – my husband was a factory worker, he's an optician now, it's a different scene, but that's another story – but he was a factory worker and he went to work in horrible overalls and boiled in the summer and came home covered in grease. I didn't want his job. Men have certain powers if they care to exercise them and a lot of them do, over women. But it has to be understood that some of the exercise of that power over women actually comes because of their outside lives, far from it being this great free expansive life that Simone de Beauvoir seemed to think all men lived. Coming home and being the lord and master was out of the same stable as coming home and kicking the cat.

It wasn't enough to recognise the oppression of women. You had also to recognise that the majority of the population was oppressed and deprived. In my book you never get an adequate woman's response which doesn't take this in. It doesn't mean that you subordinate women's struggle to it at all. It's much more complicated than that. But you certainly can't simplify it that man equals free, woman equals oppressed. It was a corrective that I felt needed to be injected.

I was a sort of walking interface between one element of struggle and another. I felt like a bridge. I was part of the trade-union movement absolutely legitimate, accepted – and I was absolutely legitimate in the Labour Party. I became involved in the women's organisation of the Labour Party, as soon as women really started taking it over. The traditional

208

women's sections in the Labour Party got less and less, because people like me didn't take part in them.

I wanted to inject the trade-union background into socialist feminism: working-class socialist feminist, shorthand typist socialist feminist, husband factory-worker socialist feminist. I don't remember what was in the paper I wrote at all. But I remember I chose an example of how you couldn't simplify things. I chose the example of the miner. I said, 'Now, which of you here will say which is the more oppressed? The miner, or the miner's wife?' And to me that's an unanswerable question. They both are. It's a pointless argument. The fact that miners can be what we would now say male chauvinist pigs, doesn't alter the fact that to be a miner was and is to have a rotten job. The fact that they've had to fight to try and keep clinging on to those jobs just shows the state we're in. The women in that hall would not have wanted to work down the pit.

I know that now there is this thing from America about women wanting to become miners – I must say I distrust it wholly. I think they're off their rockers. I know that for every woman who was going down the mine in order to show that she thought it would be an exciting or invigorating job, there would be a hundred who would be going down because they had no alternative. Just as all this stuff about working nights, and the protective legislation. We're told it holds women back. Absolute baloney. The protective legislation – the fact that women are deprived of work in certain areas has got nothing to do ·with protective legislation. Women are deprived of work and promotion prospects in all areas, including where night work is never worked, and there's no protective legislation. It is a total irrelevance. All these women who think you can't claim equality without taking the rough with the smooth are not going to be the ones who have the rough.

I picked up this idea that feminism is enough. Feminism is not enough, and I wanted to inject that into the Ruskin conference, right at the beginning. I think that people found it quite hard going. It wasn't cosy. If I'd been in a meeting of trade-union women, I'd have probably been saying, 'You can't say that these middle-class women have nothing to offer this movement.' I'd then have been going on about the contribution they'd already made, women doctors, education, and so on. I'd have been doing the reverse of the coin.

I enjoyed the weekend. I was thrilled at the size of it. That was very good. I didn't feel any kind of censure, even where I thought they were putting the wrong emphasis. I went away very friendly to it all, and I always regarded myself as part of the women's liberation movement. I tried to make a space for women's liberation in the other things that I was involved in. I never went to anything like consciousness-raising groups. Not that I disagreed with them, but you can't do everything. And my consciousness didn't need improving, or raising, it was there. I don't think there's only one way to do anything.

I became a Member of Parliament in 1974. I would have become an MP or not, regardless of the women's movement. The big change came when I became a candidate, not all that long after the Ruskin conference. The union ceased to be my main field of activity and the Labour Party itself became a bigger field. But it was quite coincidental. To be candid it was because I moved house and the union establishment then took the opportunity of making my union activity extremely difficult by putting me in a branch about forty miles from where I lived. It made it really impossible for me to be as central in union activities as I had been. They couldn't force me out but they certainly took away some of the opportunity, and that was a manipulative thing.

I became a constituency Labour Party chair, and then became a parliamentary candidate. I'd been very noisy in the 1960s with my complaints about what the Labour government did and people started to say, when they were selecting

210

candidates for 1974, 'Would you be willing?', and I felt I either had to say yes, or forever be quiet. I lived in Stafford then. I was very uneasy about it, but my husband was very much in favour. I went to three places, and I was selected on the third seat. So I was lucky. When I got into Parliament it was said 'Now we've got a Women's Lib MP'. I wouldn't have expected to categorise myself as a woman MP.

There's been a spiral, not a circle. The first women who came in, came in very much as women MPs, lots of them came in on seats that their husbands had. Lena Jeger was one of the last to do that. Her husband died, and she was elected in 1952 or so in the bye-election. There was a whole string of women who almost inherited seats from husbands. They, I think, probably were very much typecast as women MPs. So then the generation of women who came in in the 1950s, some of whom were still in when I came in, they were like I was in the union: just as I was a trade unionist, they were an MP, and their struggle was to be accepted on the same terms as men.

I remember Lena Jeger telling me about her maiden speech, and Herbert Morrison had said, 'Make it on women's issues, dear, you can't go wrong.' He meant prices, but not as an economic factor: the woman with the shopping basket. She made it on foreign policy, and he said to her afterwards, 'You didn't take my advice,' and she said, 'Don't you think peace is a women's issue?' And all those years later, twenty-two years afterwards, there was still indignation in her voice when she told me! She said, 'We hardly spoke after that.' By the time my intake came in in 1974, you were accepted. Nobody thought it was odd that I went on the Industry Bill Committee, for instance, or the Finance Bill. We were accepted fully as colleagues. Then we started to claim women's issues and assert women's issues, as defined by us.

In Parliament we started to say things like 'There's got to be more women on this committee,' and we had demonstrations. On the Select Committee in 1975, that was looking

211

at battered wives, there were two women put on and we were supposed to be grateful. We were furious. We prevented the setting up of that Select Committee for weeks and weeks, because there's machinery you can use to do that. That involved us working together as women, which was new. We demanded places on committees, and there was incredulity by the men. Having a minority in here is a cause for complaint. We were quite stroppy. I suddenly realised, I think of myself very much as representing not just my constitutents but also women in general.

I lost my seat in 1979, so I was out of Parliament for eight years. I'm not primarily a parliamentarian. Now I'm back, things are different. Before we used to have informal contact in the lady members' room, which is like a sitting-room attached to the toilet – it's quite handy to have, mind you, I'm not in favour of abolishing it. Now the Labour women meet as a Labour women's caucus, and we call it the Women's Caucus, what's more. The Black members have set up a Black Caucus. Of course, there's only four of them. But we called it the Women's Caucus first. It stretches reasonably across the political spectrum, in the Labour Party. There's a more delicate change – you're treading on eggs even to refer to it – and that is the relations between some Tory ladies and the Labour women on abortion. But in the 1970s there wasn't a single thing on which there was ever an overlap, absolutely not. The Tory ladies are incredibly Tory, and were more so then, and the Labour women tended to be radical. Any rebellion or anything progressive in this place on the Labour side, you'd find a disproportionate number of women, very markedly.

The women's movement ebbs and flows and has different strengths and different emphases at times. It's a lot more fragmented now. It started off with two very distinct strands, the trade-union working-class equal pay strand, and the 'women's lib' strand, with not many links. I was a link. They

212

went on in parallel. The women's lib side has fragmented a lot, and people got immersed in single issues like the abortion issue, for instance. It isn't one nice neat movement you can tie up with a ribbon and deliver.

Sue O'Sullivan

I probably was the most pregnant person who's ever been to a women's liberation conference! I had Dan, my second child, about ten days later. That dominates my memory of the conference; what I remember most clearly is being huge. I was quite uncomfortable, you know how you get, that kind of beached whale feeling.

I had been a dance major at college in the United States. I started in 1959, then left and came to London, then I went back. I did my final year in 1965–66. I thought I wanted to be an actress. It wasn't until I got to college that I started dancing. I loved it. It was modern dance, Merce Cunningham was my favourite; I had a kind of natural talent for dancing, but I didn't have any training. I worked very hard to get a technique. I was involved in fringe dance stuff, the kind where you walk round Washington Square (in Greenwich Village, New York) with a ladder and a bucket and nobody knows what you're doing. I think some of the people I was around with in the dance world did go on to do more political things, although I think dance is probably one of the last of the arts to get political. So self-obsessed with the body.

I came to London with two friends, one of them got into the London School of Economics. I pretended to myself and everybody else that I would get into the LSE or some place else if I just got there and went for an interview. Well, I didn't. I had enough money to live on for a year on a very low level. But one of the girls that I was with, her parents were living here in London, her father was a movie director. He directed movies like *The Three Faces of Eve*, *Gentlemen Prefer Blondes*. We found a wonderful flat in Notting Hill Gate, near Portobello Road. It's a place any of us nowadays would be proud to live in. But my friend's mother didn't think it was good enough for her daughter and we allowed her to take over. She found a basement flat off the King's Road and we paid her £3 a week while she made up the rest. It was way beyond our means.

I discovered a dance studio in Notting Hill Gate run by an independent ballet teacher, a wonderful old woman, and spent a lot of time there. I also hung around the LSE, where my friend was studying, which is how I met my husband in 1961–62. I met him at a party that we gave at the flat. It was filled up with people from the LSE where he was a graduate student. Nobody had cars. You would get on the train and go way out to somebody's place that you'd never been to before. Then you either had to rush out to get the train back, or stay over in the flat until five in the morning, when you were hungover, exhausted, and people were sleeping on the floor.

I was standing in the kitchen and we'd made all sorts of American dips – with crackers and cut up vegetables – and he walked into the kitchen, with his London accent and his donkey jacket and jeans, and said 'Don't you have any real food?' I thought, 'This is it'. And I slept with him. But we didn't do anything, we just lay on the floor in the living room with everyone else. I was struck, in love. He was the president of the Socialist Society. That year I'd gone on the big anti-nuclear Aldermaston march. In fact I got arrested in Trafalgar Square.

I'd been around Quaker stuff in the States, all pacifism and

215

ban-the-bomb. My family were Quakers; it was more organised, was more militant here. But it was very easy, especially through the connections of the LSE, to enter into that. I don't think I did get class politics that year, but I certainly was confronted with it, through people at LSE who just assumed that you lived within a class society and the way to understand that was to be a socialist or a Marxist. All this was very separate from the dance.

I went back to the United States for a year and then I came back to England and got married. I knew from the moment that I got back to the United States that I was madly in love and I wanted to come back and be with him. I was quite excited about the fact that I was going to move away from my family. We lived in his parents' house for the summer of 1963, and he was working as a farm labourer. We got married in September of 1963, and came to London. He was still a graduate student.

I located a small modern dance class at an Adult Education Institute near Euston. It was run by a man called Ernest Berk who was connected to German modern dance coming out of the thirties. He was also into concrete music. We did performances there. Out of that came a little dance company called the Emanon Dance Company – 'No Name' spelt backwards. Everybody in it was political. A woman, Becky Wilson, choreographed a dance we did at the Spanish Government in Exile's annual meeting at Conway Hall. For me it was the first time dance and politics came together in a very explicit way.

My husband finished his graduate work in 1965, and we decided that we'd go to New York, and I would go back to college, and finish my degree. Through a series of wonderful coincidences he got a job at the New School for Social Research, which he didn't realise until the day he started was in the graduate department. He'd never taught before. I went back to college.

Luckily we got a rent control flat in the Village, and we

216

had a fantastic two years there. I was doing dance, but I was also studying history and literature. I was approaching studying in a much more serious way than I had before. I had a terrific year. Then the next year I taught nursery school, which meant only a half day's work. We just assumed that we would come back to London. The two years had been terrific and politically exciting. It was new left politics, it was all SDS (Students for a Democratic Society) stuff, all of that was bubbling away. Black Power. It felt exciting in New York, being around at that point. And I was dancing at the Cunningham Studio, and that was very important to me. But also we'd decided that we'd have a baby, and I got pregnant right before we came back. I had Tom here, in 1968. (We were living in Stoke Newington. Friends at that point used to say, 'Where's that, south of the river?') I felt different I think, having come back after two years in the United States, where I had caught the flavour of political involvement. I was moved by Black Power. I wasn't involved in any particular group. I felt I was challenged personally by Black people, being compelled to reflect on my own life and my own ways of thinking, by that movement.

I went to dance classes until I was about six months pregnant. I had this illusion that I was quite slim, but I've seen pictures of myself and I now realise I was huge. So it's not really surprising that I was taken aside one day after dance class and told that I was upsetting the rest of the dancers too much. They were terrified that I was going to pop on the dance floor! I think I was a bit upset. Although I'd met a lot of new women through dance, I hadn't connected with those women as friends the way I had in the United States. I missed having close friends. I felt lonely. English people seemed difficult to get to know. I didn't know how to 'hang out' with English folk.

My husband was in fact very active. I used to go along with him, to meetings, but it was very much as an appendage. I sort of listened. I must have been taking something in, but I did feel it wasn't my thing. Then we went off to America in the summer of 1968 when Tom was three months old, and met up with old friends, and there was women's liberation floating around. I didn't really connect it to myself much. We got back to London at the end of August.

Then in autumn 1968, I went to the Tufnell Park women's group, and I never looked back. It was like pieces suddenly falling into place, like light being shed on dark places, it was like sense being made out of my individual fed-upness. It was the first time I'd ever felt any desire to be part of anything that was collective, a group. I carried around with me all that American bullshit about 'I don't like groups, I believe in individuals'. And there it was, I loved it.

I had been moved intellectually and emotionally by my own relationship to Black politics and my relation to oppression. I was challenged. I was put up against the wall as a white person. But left politics hadn't incorporated me. I didn't feel valuable. I didn't feel as if I had much to offer, and it wasn't about my life. I had suffered terribly with all sorts of insecurities around having a baby. I think it was having Tom that catapulted me into needing something. I was just in a state of shock. I couldn't come to grips with being a mother. I didn't know what it meant. It didn't give me huge amounts of joy. I didn't know whether I was doing it right. A lot of those women had kids, and we could talk about kids. I danced after Tom was born, but with less and less involvement. Until I was pregnant again with Dan, I was still dancing. In fact, I kept on dancing off and on up until, oh, maybe ten years ago.

My husband and I were both aware that we were riveted on this little child. It was literally physical sometimes, there was Tom being this delightful little solemn baby lying in the middle of the floor in the evening, for instance, and his father and I would be sitting in two chairs just staring at him. Completely fascinated. There was this child captured between two adult gazes. You felt it was maybe not the healthiest thing in the world, that it would be good to break that intensity.

I think I heard about Ruskin through the small group, I can't even remember who it was who knew about it. My husband got involved in different meetings that took place from the beginning between some of the men. It wasn't a 'men's' group. One thing we were clear about was that we were going to have a creche involving men, and the men did meet and discuss that. What to do and the toys they would have, the nappies, and all that. There was never any doubt that he was coming and Tom was coming. It was a family affair. I think there was only one other occasion when we all went to one of the big women's liberation occasions together. I quickly realised that I was much happier if I was without the children – even if they were in a creche – I liked it better when I could leave being a mother at home. I know we were supposedly being 'political' about the 'personal' and creating collective childcare, but as long as I had the choice I preferred not having to be a mother for a while. And it was soon obvious that my kids weren't enamoured by conference creches.

I enjoyed Ruskin a lot. I don't remember that much about it actually, and I don't know whether that's because I was pregnant. I didn't know many other women. I remember just standing and sitting around and talk, talk, talking. Just the big whole thing, with all the ancient male statues draped with scarves and being with that number of women. I'd never been in Oxford before. And then didn't the walls get painted up? I didn't know whether I approved or not, but I didn't think it was an awful thing to have done. I think I was generally and uncritically excited by almost every single thing that happened. I think I was right in the mood for dramatics and self-revelations. Something which felt very exciting and important.

There were women from all over, and different ages, that was the amazing thing as well. There were women who were older. Obviously like we are now. Been around for years, but it had all died away. It was the excitement of being there at the beginning of something that was going to get huge. I don't think I felt at that point that it was going to change the world overnight. But I couldn't imagine that lots and lots of women weren't going to be compelled in the same way. It wasn't as if you were 'better' or 'different' from other women and that's why you were at Ruskin, more that you were lucky to have heard about it so soon.

I wanted a girl. The doctor said to me, 'Don't worry, it's a wonderful son, you can have a girl next time.' I said, 'There won't be a next time.' And I really meant it. But I was disappointed. I really wanted to have a girl. Now I don't feel regretful. I think it would have meant very different things in my life if I'd had a girl. I don't think I could have upped and left my little nest of men. I don't think I would have been able to work through my guilt about that as much.

The literal picking up and going didn't happen till six years ago. The leaving on some levels happened when I started having relationships with women, in 1976–7.

I suffered with post-natal depression with Dan in a way that I never had with Tom. I had a very very easy birth with Dan, he popped out so easily. With Tom I'd been in labour for two days. But with Dan afterwards I thought I was never going to surface. I felt unable to express it to anyone. I couldn't call up my women's group and say, 'Get over here.' People maybe brought flowers round, but I was back in the nuclear family, and I couldn't get out. I was just a mess; for three months seriously, and then less and less. I was aware of it but I think I blamed it on myself.

I couldn't tell my doctor about it. I'd go in to see the doctor and I'd end up smiling cheerfully, which is very much the way that I might be now too. A tendency to be cheery and to smile, and be self-deprecating and all that. So I was unable to express this. My husband knew just how desperate I was. He told me afterwards that he was afraid to leave me on my own sometimes. Then I started going again to women's groups, to the meetings. I think before that I got involved in Camden Movement for People's Power. We had a little Saturday thing with kids. It was anti-Vietnam war and taking up issues like childcare and creches. It was also having this rather scruffy little place open and having people come in, based on the American community politics.

Later, Maiden Lane community site involved a number of women and there was a women's centre in Essex Road around the same time. When the kids were about one and three I started reading books about China and then Mao himself. We had this ideal of working, drawing in local women. There was nothing formal. Nobody belonged to a Maoist group. There was no question that any of us were involved in any one of the sectarian groups around at that time. But we were, in the same way as a lot of people in 1968 were, in love with the cultural revolution. All those things, being on *Red Rag*, (the Marxist Women's Liberation magazine), and being in the Marxist study groups, the women's centres, on the community centre site, seemed to me like that was it. It felt as if we were at least attempting to live out theory and practice.

I suppose it ties into the history of Quakers being 'do-gooders'. But I was in flight from its individualism and liberalism. It's weird because my parents are liberals, but as Quakers and liberals in the United States they were, as I was growing up in the fifties, in a very oppositional position. It seems bizarre if you measure their politics round what we would call radical. In many ways they aren't radical, but in America they were oppositional to the Republican party that was dominant in the town I grew up in, oppositional to being in the armed forces; my father had been a conscientious objector. Liberal about race. No class politics at all. For the forties and fifties that was quite a different thing.

For about two or three years I was feeling very constrained and very weighed down with these two little kids. If I look at

221

myself physically in pictures of that time, well, I remember feeling bedraggled, unwashed hair, drudge. Tired. I wasn't going to dance classes regularly, but I would go along as often as I could. I stopped being serious about dance, from 1969 on – when I talk about going back to dance classes after that, it's not with any idea that I was going to be a dancer – there was a point after I got involved in women's liberation where I knew that given the choice to be off on a demonstration or be in a dance studio, there's no question about where I wanted to be. I was also getting more and more critical of a kind of narcissism of a lot of dancers.

I don't think at that point that you thought about taking women's liberation into your profession, your chosen area. It was more like your life was being changed and you were meeting other women on a very personal ground. It wasn't about art, for me. Dancers are incredible; they literally do their training in front of mirrors. They are riveted, locked into it – you go into a dance studio and you see them. Or else there's an edge of looking round in a kind of competitive way. There's something quite exaggerated about it. Also, I thought I had a big pot belly.

I went to China in 1974. I was fascinated with the politics. I did think this was something to see at work. I think I had a bit of a thing from my parents, you know, that travel is the finest form of improvement. I felt elated by the experience. Then I got involved in SACU (Society for Anglo-Chinese Understanding) and I got more into community projects because I got involved with the local tenants association. For a time we had a Marxist study group. There were six of us, four working-class men and women and two middle-class women, including me. We used to read *Peking Reviews*, Mao, Marx and Lenin. In fact it was wonderful. We would read out loud and discuss a different text each week.

These different things didn't all have the same politics. The women's stuff didn't have the socialism, the socialism didn't have the feminism, the family thing had me shrieking

222

and screaming and being an absolute bitch. But I don't get bored, never get bored. I've only been bored maybe two dozen times in my life.

I can see connections between things, but none of them would have had the same meaning if I hadn't got involved in women's liberation. That meant everything. And because I got involved in that such a short time before Ruskin, Ruskin was an entry port. I had my small group, but Ruskin was like the big wide world. It was an introduction. For me the class-based politics was what I'd been confronted with or learned about: I had to have women's liberation for myself. I don't mean I had to be liberated, I had to be involved in that as a person. It was my movement. As opposed to someone else's: It was only after feeling confident about that and having that as a perspective on the way the world worked, that I could then approach class politics, and socialism. From my own ground.

I discovered in my first relationship with a woman that I hadn't been a lesbian all along, but I sure as hell wanted to be one from that point on; it was like a blinding flash. I hadn't realised how big a change that would mean sexually, and how much of a revelation it would be to me. From that point on I think there was a real struggle in myself because I really knew where my heart lay, as far as sexuality went, but also I had so much good history and current love for my husband and I had the two kids who I felt passionate about.

So for the next few years, there was a real struggle within myself to try and work something out so that I wouldn't hurt anyone. Obviously I was always hurting someone by having other relationships. I didn't want to be selfish but I didn't want to sacrifice myself either.

I worked on *Spare Rib* for five years. It took over my life. From 1977 to 1978 I did a Health Education Diploma, because I'd been teaching health in Holloway Prison, and then the job for *Spare Rib* just popped up. It seemed absolutely the right thing to do. I'd loved being on *Red Rag*, which I left in

223

the mid-seventies. When I was on that I liked thinking about it, when it would come out, having to remember this and writing notes on that. I think I was a real bossy boots and very moralistic around it. I began to get crabbier and crabbier as the years went on, in that self-righteous way that you can, if you feel you've taken hold of something, and are responsible.

I think it was around the *Red Rag* time that I, and other women who were involved in the same things, really jumped into Marxism and study groups and were honing our positions, our political positions, as Marxists. At that time we were very sharply attuned to anything that the Communist Party was doing and also thought we could see practically the way that they were working, and it didn't seem straightforward. Like at conferences where the CP women would say they weren't there as CP women, but they would caucus together. They wouldn't admit they were caucussing together, they would only all happen to be having breakfast together. I remember wanting to have articles and discussions on Ireland, wanting the broad spectrum of issues, believing that we could address anything, and being told by other women on *Red Rag* that wasn't an issue for women's liberation. We never ever really sat down and engaged with what was going on.

I'd always had a suspicion of organised parties and then when I wanted to join one I couldn't find the right one. They were reformist, or sectarian, or ultra left and none convinced me about their commitment to women's liberation. The community politics that I *was* involved in, in terms of class or women's stuff, had as an ideal locally-based projects and organising. Then at *Spare Rib* you sat up in an office in Clerkenwell Close, and were definitely not directly involved in any community, you were in an office. You had a constituency, and if you had any principles I think you attempted to keep in contact with that constituency. But I think also there was a cutting off. There wasn't time. I stopped the community politics, although off and on I was involved in various things, health stuff, helping to organise women's health conferences.

I don't dance now, not at all. I'd love to, because there's nothing like a wonderful dance class, it's just joyful – if I can feel my body understanding it. If it's really difficult for me and I can't do it and I'm frustrated by it, I end up in tears. Well, I used to. But I never could find a studio which was easy to get to, where I loved the classes enough. Some of the classes I went to at the early dance centres felt like factories, there wasn't much joy. All that fake jazz dancing. I'm sure I could have found something but it wasn't easy – to find the intensity on a casual basis. I gave up at a certain point, you see, even though I taught dance in Holloway for a number of years. I like being in a class with a particular kind of teacher, one who is very encouraging, engaged, but can teach, can convey both the technique and the expression. And where you have accompaniment that is good, rhythm that's good. I miss it, except I get some of the same pleasure going out dancing, just going to clubs.

As for women's liberation, it's still there, still my bedrock, only it doesn't seem so big now, more like an island maybe. Bridges figure much more prominently. I've changed, the world's changed and of course it's not a simple thing. It never was. Maybe it's easier as a lesbian, although I can hear snorts at that!

Sometimes I'm nervous that I just hold on because to let go would be so terrible, but then a kind of confidence reasserts itself. What's so great about cynicism? I want to be worldly but hold on to a belief in the possibility of change. To be cynical is to be bored, to be half way to defeat. OK, in many ways things are going backwards now. But I know what I knew at Ruskin, that the way we live in the world as women isn't any more natural than a 3D movie. Nothing stays static.

I saw my own relationship to the world change through

women's liberation. It was a good change and it wasn't simply about me as an individual. That stays with me as I live through the years. As depressing, right wing and reactionary as things are, I feel lucky. Of course it's not fashionable and may sound naive, but I've had so much pleasure through feminism, so much intensity and heart-thudding engagement. Pain too but pleasure's won out so far.

As I come towards fifty I'm subject to more anxiety about my material welfare. I'm not secure in my low-paid job nor in short-life housing and I have periods of wondering if I should have paid more attention to those things. There is a pressure around to fold back on yourself, think about security, success, settle down, and I'm not immune to it. But in general I don't regret not having those things. Recently I've begun to think of everything good which may still come my way as a bonus, plusses on top of a very fortunate base. Does that sound crazy? I suppose it's a way of living more from month to month, year to year. We grow older.

Women's liberation gave me energy, sometimes discouragement but so far the energy always comes back. I fuck up. I weep on my own at the horrors of the world. I get depressed. I shout at the television when the news is on. I also get moved deeply by peoples' courage, their resistance, by nature, colours, by my children, friends, lover.

I thought that women's liberation was a beginning, for women and for me personally. I've learned a lot since then: I know now what I didn't know then, that women had been feminists long before our 'wave'. But for me it was a beginning. If it were only a duty, an empty promise, I think the bleakness would overwhelm me, but you see I still believe deeply in justice and in those rhetorical things like an end to exploitation and oppression. How could they ever be boring or unfashionable? And who says you can't dance too?

Appendix

Women and the Family

Jan Williams, Hazel Twort and Ann Bachelli

(This paper was written by members of the London Peckham Rye group, Women's Liberation Workshop, and presented at the Ruskin College Women's Conference, Oxford, March 1970. It was also printed in *Shrew*, February–March 1970.)

This paper has been written by three women, each with two kids. We talked and wrote together as a group. We are oppressed and have been from the moment we were born. Our families have squashed us into roles because our mothers wanted daughters in their own image, and our fathers wanted daughters like their submissive wives. We each had a *girlhood* instead of a childhood and are only now beginning to be conscious of what that means in terms of what we are now. Now we feel we are martyrs. Martyrdom that has, over the years of being housewives and mothers, become almost enjoyable. The family exists on martyrdom. This is generally getting less but only since we have glimpsed how we live from outside. We have found it extremely difficult to look at ourselves – as through a window – and most of all it has been a sheer impossibility to imagine ourselves being involved in change of any sort. Our window on the world is looked through with our hands in the sink and we've begun to *hate that sink and all it implies – so begins our consciousness.* We need to work, work is a dignity, or should be, we know that most work is not, but at least at worst it involves you with other people, ideas and a struggle. Women are still told that they are oppressed because of capitalism: get rid of that and it'll all be alright. But this serves no purpose at all to women who don't feel part of anything, it *just pushes them further away from ever feeling anything.* The oppression every woman suffers is deeply in her, she first has to realise this and then to fight it – with other women helping. Men will not generally help with this, they need passive, ignorant, decorative women. We are, therefore, talking about that 65 per cent of women who do not work and who are presumably housewives.

The 'family', as it is experienced, is the woman and the children *in* the house, the flat or the room and the man who comes and goes. The space that the family occupies is essential to its own image of itself, its own way of living, its self-expression. The woman who goes out to work goes out of her family if only for that period of time: however drab the work routine, children are temporarily forgotten, housework ignored. *In the home* the woman is *in the family*, and the two are disturbingly synonymous. Housework cannot be separated from children, nor the children from the four walls, the food you cook, the shopping you do, the clothes you wear. How you, the house, the children, *look* may not be how they are, but reflects what you want them to be. It is not just that every pop-psychologist's 'mum' lives in a *Woman's Own* dreamhouse, where the material solution to any problem is immediately on hand; it is that in our society being a mother is being a housewife: the security of the family is the stability of the walls – the image of the family home is the image of the family, but not in any simple way. The folklore has many permutations – from happy secure family in new semi, to poor but happy slum dwellers, to the 'broken home' of the 'juvenile delinquent' who comes from both.

There is little to be said about housework on its own. An endless routine, it creates its own high moments of achievement and satisfaction so as to evade not monotony – the feature of many jobs – but *futility*. The bolt you tighten on the factory floor vanishes to be replaced by another: but the clean kitchen floor is tomorrow's dirty floor and the clean floor of the day after that. The appropriate symbol for housework (and for housework *alone*) is not the interminable conveyor-belt but a compulsive circle like a pet mouse in its cage spinning round on its exercise wheel, unable to get off. Into this one inserts one's own saving peaks: 'happiness is the bathroom scrubbed down'. But even the glorious end of today's chores is not even an anti-climax as there *is* no real *climax* – there is nothing to fill the 'joyful moment'. But the routine is never quite routine, so the vacuum in one's mind is never vacuous enough to be filled. 'Housework is a worm eating away at one's ideas.' Like a fever dream it goes on and on, until you desperately hope that it can all be achieved at one blow. You lay the breakfast the night before, you have even been known to light the gas under the kettle for tomorrow's tea, wishing that by breakfast time everything could be over with – by 8 a.m. The children washed, teeth-cleaned and ready for bed, tucked-up, *the end*.

And yet there is nothing tangible to force you to do it. A job is compulsory: either you go or you don't have a job. The pressures of housework are more insidious: neighbours criticise and compare; grandmothers hand on standards; within you and without you is your mother's voice, criticising and directing. Their overriding criterion is cleanliness: a dirty house is a disintegrating person. The compulsion to housework, then, is not economic or legal: it is moral and personal. And the housewife sees it in moral and personal terms. Hence her description of this structure of her oppression assumes querulous and complaining tones, the tones of a private neurosis to express

229

a social fact – the imposed isolation of her work. For emancipated women to attack the complaint and ignore the whole socialising force which produces it simply reinforces the position. Like every other form of social activity, every other aspect of social relationships, housework cannot be pinned down to a neat descriptive formula. The more we examine it, the more aspects it reveals, and the more we become aware of its contradictions and paradoxes. Isolated, the only adult in a private house, the housewife is yet crowded, by the emotional and physical demands of her family, by the unseen pressures of society. But although isolated, the housewife is never alone: her domain is the kitchen, the most communal room, and even the possibility of sleeping alone is denied her. To have the right to sleep alone is essential. People in permanent relationships do not do this. A woman needs time alone – after a day of being a public servant to the rest of the family, of giving out all the time, of being open to all demands – and in ordinary families the only time of the day this feeling of aloneness is possible is during the few moments before she goes to sleep after getting into bed. To then have to touch, caress, console yet another person is too much. The hatred of the man and sex begins – it is the beginning of such sayings as 'Oh God, he wants his rights again' or the husband saying 'you can't have a headache every night'. So that eventually she has no identity, no specificity, no privacy – she is defined by the demands of others. The only escape is the daydream, turning-in-on-oneself is the only way out. It is a journey from a body which is always being touched – the mother must always allow herself to be open to physical contact – to an area which cannot be touched, to an area of total privacy, where one's body is one's own again. Ironically, housework is often seen as being self-determined labour – 'your time is your own'. In fact, in order to 'keep up', in order to be 'a good housewife', one has to work to a pre-determined routine. The 'freedom' of the housewife is in fact the denial of her right to a job. Even the division work/place of work, leisure/home does not apply to the housewife: her place of work is also the

230

place of leisure and further it is her work which provides the basis of other people's leisure.

The 'rationalisation' of housework is held out as a future prospect – better technical equipment means less work. But even if this different equipment were made easily available to all classes, the situation of the housewife would be essentially unchanged, and problems would remain. Indeed some would be exacerbated. The only social world most housewives have is the shopping centre – hence their 'irrational' tendency to shop every day rather than once a week. Deprived of this they would lose one way of keeping up their morale. Being literally house-bound, afraid of leaving the house and being seen is a typical woman's syndrome. Developments in technology on their own cannot change women's position in the home. We must be quite clear about this.

Unless we can discuss through the implications of the role of the housewife – the *institution* of the housewife, if you like – and work out the reasons why this institution survives so tenaciously, we will be unable to combat the various levels of oppression. Moreover, it is not enough simply to command women out to work – particularly since we all know that means that women usually end up with two jobs, one monotonous, the other futile.

We would like at this point to make clear that we do hold our children very dear. We love them passionately and care deeply about them. We feel it is because of this, or at least with this as one of the main reasons, that we have become immersed in working for the liberation of women.

Women are brought up for marriage and motherhood. The essential time spent in this is five years – five out of a lifetime of seventy years and more. The discrepancy between the time spent and the importance given to it is understandable – the human infant *does* need much care and attention. But from the viewpoint of the woman the discrepancy is absurd. Her whole life seems to be one long 'before' and 'after'. Children go on being children beyond their first five years, in fact often until

231

they produce the grandchildren which can replace them in their mother's eyes. But what does being a mother mean? In modern mythology it means a consistent being, untouched by the moods which the child exhibits, always forgiving, understanding, and certainly never violent or moody. The tyranny of consistency undermines both mother – she must never give way to anger or even to sudden affection – and child – whatever it does the superior adult can cope. It sets in motion a circular pattern. Consistency eventually means monotony; inconsistency leads to guilt; both cover suppressed feelings which can erupt into violence – which itself once more produces guilt and the struggle for the elusive and magical consistency. The smooth, unruffled exterior is simultaneously a masking of and a cause of conflict. Modern notions of the perfect and well-adjusted mother must be questioned and challenged. It may well be that they are designed not only to produce a compliant child, but also to produce the mother who, by turning a serene and contented face to the world, gives it an alibi for ignoring her problem.

Guilt and anxiety always weave their way through one's happiness. The guilt of giving birth is endorsed by the constant notion that you are responsible for the child's personality. The first months of a baby's life are full of difficulties – the lack of sleep, the fear (particularly with the first child) that you are not doing the right thing, the appalling ignorance and one's amateur status. The only answer to these problems appears to be total dedication to the child. Furthermore, this dedication can be seen as an investment in the child's future – at least one might prevent future neuroses. Even more, your anxiety can cover up feelings of violence and hatred towards your child. The mother of the battered baby acts out the fantasies of many mothers. And however anti-authoritarian the mother hopes to be in the future, or for that matter in the present, she still wants the children to do what she wants them to do.

For some families, one route out of the problem of the all-embracing mother and the pressures upon her has been a shifting of roles. The father has entered more into the life of the child. But this shifting of roles had also been a subtle reversal of roles. Instead of the comforting mother, whose ultimate threat was always 'I'll tell your father', and the punitive father, the father has become the source of amusement, and the mother has remained the person ultimately responsible for the child's psychological and emotional future. Although the roles have changed, the ultimate responsibility has remained unchanged.

For this reason we should not be misled into thinking that the simple extension of woman into the man's role and the man into the woman's is the solution of the problem. Man as mother as well as man as house-slave is no answer. Obviously men can, and should, (and in rare cases do) perform domestic tasks and bring up families. This is not the point at issue. In the end the demand for complete reversal is the demand to extend oppression – understandable, but leading to a dead end. Our perspective must be different.

The demand for communal living must be understood in this way. The commune offers obvious advantages – at the minimum it helps to spread the load, to share work and thus to allow us time which is really free. But we must be careful not to turn it into an extended family, turned in on itself, where all are enclosed in increasing domesticity.

We must also be aware of its limitations. Living communally can only change the lives of the people in the community. It can help people to become less obsessed about their possessions and help them to regard their children in a less possessive way. It could help people out economically and offer them a less competitive home environment. It can free women a little to pursue their own work by sharing the practicalities of daily living. What it cannot do is be anything more than an individual solution to an individual's neuroses. The causes of these neuroses will still be present and real to all around her and thereby to her. Living in a commune must not be envisaged as a resolution of the housewife problem. The crucial point is that however women live in this society, their militant work must be governed by the imperative need to rouse the consciousness of their silent, submerged sisters. Women must realise the deadly effects of their passivity and overcome them by working together for their liberation.

Identity

Dinah Brooke

(Written by a member of the London Women's Liberation Workshop, and presented as a talk to students at Hornsey College of Art in Summer 1971, as part of a series of seminars on Women's Studies)

Who are you? Who am I? I'm Dinah Brooke. I'm a writer. No, I'm not. I'm Dinah Dux, wife of an American, mother of twins. Well, I'm both. Anyway, I'm Dinah. Brooke is my father's surname. Dux is my husband's surname.

Of course, it doesn't really mean anything when you change your name when you get married. It just means you've promised to obey somebody. A man. You chose him though. You chose who you were going to obey, so that makes it all right really. It was a free choice. Oh, it also means you can't buy a house unless he signs the papers, or have the coil fitted without his written consent, and things like that, because after all he's a man, and he's responsible for you.

But these are external things, nothing to do with your real identity, are they? I mean, you know who you are really. You

235

feel who you are. You are what you feel. But then you feel different at different times. If you've been to a cousin's wedding, perhaps, or seen a sentimental film, you might suddenly be overwhelmed by a sentimental desire for white veils and orange blossom, and a little log cabin, and homebaked bread, and a babe on your knee. Or perhaps it was a different sort of film and you feel irresistably attractive and doomed. Or perhaps you have been working well, and people like what you do, and you feel a great surge of power and energy, or perhaps you feel utterly depressed and hopeless and dull and empty. Whatever feelings you have about yourself you are not what you feel at any one moment, but a mixture of all the things you ever feel about yourself, even if they are totally contradictory. Your identity is made up of all the things you have ever felt about yourself. Even if you haven't felt them for a long time, they have still left their mark on you.

Of course there is another side to your identity too, and that is the way you appear to other people. Your parents probably have a fairly clear idea of what you are like, and could describe you quite easily. Maybe you would agree with their description, and maybe you wouldn't even recognise it. Your friends too know, to a certain extent, what you are like. They know who you are. And one of the first things they know about you is your sex. That's also one of the first things your lovers are likely to know. It was probably the first thing that was said about you when you were born. 'It's a boy', or 'It's a girl'. Your identity was first defined by your sex.

As you grew up you didn't just grow up in a vacuum. You grew up into a series of expectations. Other people's expectations about you. These are very important. Infants who are brought up in institutions where no one has much time to expect anything from them have a very high mortality rate. Children are expected to walk when they are about one, talk when they are about two, and go to school when they are five. There's a law about going to school when you are five. There isn't one about walking when you're one, but most people do it anyway. On the whole little girls are given pink baby clothes and little dresses to wear, and little boys blue baby clothes and shorts or trousers. On the whole little girls play with dolls and little boys with cars and guns. They may want to anyway, but certainly if you go into a toyshop and ask for a toy suitable for a girl you will be shown a doll, doll's house, nurse's outfit; and for a boy planes, cars, guns and cowboy suits. That's what grandparents expect of them. That's what it says in the magazines.

In school girls will probably be expected to do cooking and needlework, and boys woodwork. Girls will play hockey and rounders, boys football and cricket. When they are about fifteen most girls will probably leave school. After all, there's not much point in them getting any more education because what'll they do with it? Just get married. They might as well be earning a bit of money. They need money for clothes because boys expect them to look nice. If they stay on at school their friends will think they're right twits for still wearing some kind of horrible uniform, and never having time to go out with boys because of their homework. And as for staying on and trying to get a place at university, well, they'll have to be very bright, because the people who run the universities don't expect that many girls will want to go, so they don't provide so many places. And of course all the ones who do go are probably all doing the same subjects, English literature, or history, or art, and making things even more difficult for each other. Because when they started to specialise at school the teachers probably thought the arts were more suitable subjects for girls. I mean, why would a girl want to do mathematics or physics unless she was absolutely determined to be a doctor or a scientist, and not many people really know what they want to do at that age, or know what to do in order to do what they want.

Well, whether you've been to university and got a BA or to typing school and learned to be a secretary, you'll probably get married after a couple of years, so it really doesn't much matter what sort of job you have in between. Of course men have to get married as well. I mean obviously you can't have women getting married without men getting married. When he gets married he has to have a steady job, and a house, and be capable of supporting a wife and kids. He's got a lot of responsibilities. He'd better stick to his job and work hard at it. When she gets married she has a man who has a job and a house. She'd better work hard at keeping the house clean, and cooking tasty meals, and buying the right things. She's his wife. That's how she's identified. And then she has a kid and she's a mum. She has another to keep it company, or by mistake, or because she can't think of anything else to do, and she's still a mum. That's her identity.

What I've been trying to show in this oversimplified life history is that our identity is not decided or created entirely from within ourselves. To a very large extent it is imposed on us from outside. By other people in particular, like our parents and schoolteachers, and by other people in general. By society. Look through the advertisements in any magazine and you will see what society expects women to be like. Pretty, sexy, silly, childish, inefficient. When they are mums they know how many cans of baked beans to buy. They know about Oxo cubes. They have the whitest washing in the street, and they are always there.

You have made it as far as being students. You are probably thinking I'm different. I'm not that sort of woman. I'm intelligent and free, and my life is not going to be like that. It's quite possible that all your life you've been different from other girls. Boring, unambitious girls. Stupid cow-like women. Probably your friends and relations, fathers and boyfriends have agreed that you are different.

But the inescapable fact is that you're a woman. For people who don't know you and know that you are different, people in shops for instance, or men who whistle at you in the street, the one thing that they do know about you is that you are a woman.

So you're put in a very difficult position when you think about your identity. You are a woman. But you are not like most other women: women in advertisements for instance, or in magazine stories, or perhaps friends of your parents. You are not that sort of woman. You probably rather despise them. But what exactly is the difference? What was mum before she was identified as a mum? What was a wife before she was identified as a wife? Those words surely can't describe their real identity, their true selves, their whole selves. They are fitting into roles which society has prepared for them, and it's easy to feel rather contemptuous of them because the roles are so narrow. But it's not very pleasant to feel that people are contemptuous of you. It's a bit frightening, especially when you can see no way out of your own limited role. You probably envy the freedom of women who are not yet wives and mothers, but you daren't even admit it to yourself, so you probably react by feeling contemptuous of them and pitying the loneliness of their lives. So here are two groups of women despising each other. One for being cows and cabbages, the other for being, perhaps, promiscuous bitches, or hard and cold.

Women's Liberation Workshop Statement (1970)

WOMEN'S LIBERATION WORKSHOP believes that women in our society are oppressed. We are economically oppressed; in jobs we do full work for half pay, in the home we do unpaid work full time. We are commercially exploited by advertisements, television, and the press. Legally women are discriminated against. We are brought up to feel inadequate; educated to narrower horizons than men. This is our specific oppression as women. It is as women therefore that we are organising.

The Women's Liberation Workshop questions women's roles and redefines the possibilities. It seeks to bring women to a full awareness of the meaning of their inferior status and to devise methods to change it. In society women and girls relate primarily to men; any organisation duplicates this pattern: the men lead and dominate, the women submit.

We close our meetings to men to break through this pattern, to establish our own groups and to meet each other over our common experience as women. We want eventually to be, and to help other women to be, in charge of our own lives. Therefore, we must be in charge of our own movement – directly, not by remote control. This means that not only those with experience in politics but all must learn to take their own decisions, both political and personal.

We reject a structure based on the concept of leaders and led. For this reason, groups small enough for all to take part in discussion are basic units of our movement. We feel that the small group makes personal commitment a possibility and a necessity and that it provides understanding and solidarity. Each small group is autonomous, holding different positions and engaging in different types of activity. As a federation of a number of different groups, Women's Liberation Workshop is essentially heterogeneous, incorporating within it a wide range of opinions and plans for action. We come together as groups and individuals to further our part in the struggle for social changes and the transformation of society.

The Four Demands

At the first national women's conference at Ruskin College, Oxford, in February-March 1970, the following four demands were formulated.

EQUAL PAY
We have to understand *why* we don't have equal pay. It's always been said that a woman's place is in the home. We don't want to do equal work and housework as well. We don't want to do equal work when it's shitwork. Equal pay means not just the same money for the same work, but also recognising how many women work not because they want to, but because they *have* to, either for money or for friends. Equal pay is the first step not just to more money, but to control over how, why, and for whom we work.

EQUAL EDUCATION AND OPPORTUNITY
We don't want to demand an education equally as bad as that of men – we want equal resources, not equal repression. We want to fight for real education, to make our own jobs and opportunities.

24–HOUR NURSERIES
We need somewhere for the kids, but we have to choose as to whether the kids will be kept out of the way or given their own

space, and whether, freed from children, we just manage to survive through working or make the time to discover who stops us from living.

FREE CONTRACEPTION AND ABORTION ON DEMAND

We want to be free to choose when and how many kids to have, if any. We have to fight for control over our own bodies, for even the magic pill or (in the case of mistakes) abortion on demand only gives us the freedom to get into a real mess without any visible consequences. We still can't talk of sex as anything but a joke or a battle-ground.

(Women's Newspaper, issue no. 1, March 6 1971)

Other Virago books of interest

TRUTH, DARE OR PROMISE
Girls Growing Up in the Fifties

Edited by Liz Heron

'An absorbing, meticulous, beautifully written anthology of richly various remembered girlhoods in the optimistic days of the early Welfare State. In its pleasurable way an important piece of social history. I read with delight and recognition' — *Angela Carter*

In this superb collection of autobiographical writing, twelve women who grew into feminism in the 1970s look back on their childhoods. Some grew up in homes of pinching poverty, others in an orderliness so unbending as to be drab, still others in an easy security. In feeling, circumstance, class and culture, their experiences were as diverse as they were keenly felt. But the common feature of this post-war Britain of 'you never had it so good' were the two great landmarks of the Welfare State and the Education Act. It gave to many of these girlhoods, so like and yet so unlike those of their mothers, a sense of possibility, of aspiration to a different future. These are intimate, personal memoirs, ordinary and impossible stories that remind us how individual lives are shaped in infinitely complex ways.

VERY HEAVEN

Looking Back at the 1960s

Edited by Sara Maitland

When the Beatles hit the charts and the mini skirt hit the streets, the world changed. Or so it seemed. Twenty years on, twenty-five women look back on their lives during the decade known as the 'swinging sixties', to the challenging days of protest and pop, and the first stirrings of the Women's Liberation Movement. Their engagingly personal memoirs describe the sheer fun and excitement of those heady times as the euphoria — and the uncertainties — of new freedoms, new struggles: the 'it-changed-my-life' liberation of the Pill; Barbara Castle's days as a Cabinet Minister; trying to be a Twiggy look-alike; the eruption of the underground press with *Oz* and *Ink*; Paris and Derry in 1968; Julie Christie recalling *Darling*. For many women, it was also a decade of not belonging, of outsiderness: here are Terri Quaye's and Lee Kane's accounts of being Black in Rachman's London, and, in Uganda, Yasmin Alibhai's realis-ation that Brixton wasn't 'home'. For Michelene Wandor 'the sixties was a time when many people went to pot/except for me/I did not/. . . I yearned a lot'. These fascinating pieces, combined with Sara Maitland's perceptive and witty introduction, make *Very Heaven* a wonderful social document.

OUT THE OTHER SIDE
Contemporary Lesbian Writing

Edited by Christian McEwen and Sue O'Sullivan

In *Out the Other Side*, a collection of essays, interviews, speeches and articles, letters and journal entries, all the contributors identify as lesbian — and proudly so! — but the issues covered are by no means exclusive. There is, for example, not a single 'coming out' story. Instead the emphasis rests on the 'other side' of being out. Once a woman defines herself as lesbian, how does it affect all the other choices in her life? How does a lesbian think about sex, about families and children, about race or class or money or work, about incest or alcoholism, health or disability?

Here, thirty-five writers, half of them British, half of them North American, attempt to answer these questions. Among them are: Gloria Anzuldúa, Berta Freistadt, Meiling Jin, Audre Lorde, Sigrid Nielsen, Lisa Saffron, Marg Yeo, and many more. Their experiences vary tremendously. But always there is something of a shared tone, an urgency, an engagement. It is the tone of those who know their own situation well enough to reach beyond it, whose wish to describe is also a decision to act so that ultimately, in Irena Klepfisz's words, 'distances dissolve and differences are nourished'.

BALANCING ACTS

On Being a Mother

Edited by Katherine Gieve

'I feel I live in a constant state of surprise and suspense. It is like reading the best of novels, combined with being in love. I want things to stand still yet can't wait to see what will happen next. And, above all, I don't want the story to end.'

Thirteen women explore motherhood in this eloquent and moving book. Joy and fascination, uncertainties and ambivalences, run as common threads, as does the persistent grip of wanting to be the 'perfect mother'. There are recurring questions and a wide variety of responses. How do children change women's lives? Do you, must you, become another person when you have a child? How do women who care for children also look after their own needs and desires? Can we balance children and work? How much do fathers engage in parenting?

The circumstances in which these women are bringing up their children vary hugely, their pleasure and difficulties ranging over the whole gamut of experience. Many speak of society's disregard for the needs of mothers, both over practical matters and deeper needs. This remarkably candid book tells us much about a state 'both more overwhelming and entrancing than I could have dreamed'. The contributors are Yasmin Alibhai, Gillian Darley, Helena Kennedy, Hilary Land, Rahila Gupta, Katherine Gieve, Victoria Hardie, Elizabeth Peretz, Jean Radford, Margaret Smith, Jennifer Uglow, Julia Vellacott and Elizabeth Wilson.

DEMOCRACY IN THE KITCHEN
Regulating Mothers and Socialising Daughters

Valerie Walkerdine and Helen Lucey

How are daughters raised, how are mothers made to be 'proper' mothers and what does all this have to do with democracy? From the post-war period, with its emphasis on expanding educational possibilities for all children, to equal opportunities in the 1970s and '80s, the prevailing notion has been that 'natural' mothering (for how could it be otherwise?) would produce 'normal' children, fit for the new democratic age. These ideas have become commonsense ones, but at what cost to the lives of women? Valerie Walkerdine and Helen Lucey explore these effects by examining a well-known study of four-year-olds with their mothers, and in doing so, they tell us a different story about the divides of class and gender and the consequent social inequalities. The authors argue that, although ideas from developmental psychology are held to be progressive, they serve to support the view that there is something wrong with working-class mothering which could be put right by making it more middle-class. But nor is the middle-class home one of happy normality: in both classes, women are differently but oppressively, regulated. In this provocative book, the authors call for a new feminist engagement with class and gender socialisation to constitute a new politics of difference.